FRANCE

Maxwell A. Smith, Guerry Professor of French, Emeritus
The University of Chattanooga
Former Visiting Professor in Modern Languages
The Florida State University

EDITOR

Jacques Audiberti

TWAS 550

JACQUES AUDIBERTI

By CONSTANTIN TOLOUDIS

University of Rhode Island

TWAYNE PUBLISHERS
A DIVISION OF G. K. HALL & CO., BOSTON

Library of Congress Cataloging in Publication Data

Toloudis, Constantin.
Jacques Audiberti.

(Twayne's world authors series; TWAS 550: France)
Bibliography: pp. 146–50
Includes index.
1. Audiberti, Jacques, 1899–1965—Criticism and interpretation.
I. Title.
PQ2601.U346Z89   842'.9'12   79-9878
ISBN 0-8057-6392-9

Contents

About the Author

The author is an Associate Professor of French at the University of Rhode Island where he has been teaching French language and literature since 1966. He holds a B.A. degree from the University of British Columbia and a Ph.D. degree from Rice University. He is a former head of the Section of French Studies at the University of Rhode Island and currently the foreign language editor of *Modern Language Studies*, the journal of the North East Modern Language Association.

Preface

No one could have thought it possible in 1946, the year Audiberti's first play was produced on the stage, that the day would come when a comprehensive study would be introducing the author of *Quoat-Quoat* to an American public! In those days, it was not certain this type of theater could ensure the author's reputation even in France. Yet the fortunes of the playwright from Antibes changed rapidly on the Left Bank. Today his theater is known in more respectable quarters of the French capital, as much as it is known in the French provinces and in foreign countries like Belgium and Germany. A French production of *Quoat-Quoat* was finally brought to New York several times, for a French speaking audience which can always be counted on to be on hand in the American supermetropolis.

The star of Audiberti rose steadily through the events of his career as a dramatist. It continued to shine long after he had all but renounced his status of an avant-garde writer. The image of the playwright of the 1940's and 1950's was to be enhanced with infusions of new and unexpected glamour, in 1963, when a charismatic director, Marcel Maréchal, masterminded and executed a triumphant production of *Le Cavalier seul*, at the Théâtre du Cothurne, in Lyon. It was a fateful moment. From then on nothing would be the same. More successes of this type followed with productions of his works at the Festival du Marais, at Bourges, at Avignon. In 1976 an Audiberti colloquium was held at the prestigious center of Cerisy-la-Salle, under the direction of the indefatigable Jean-yves Guérin. This time, a wide spectrum of poets, scholars and academics engaged in erudite, often stimulating intellectual exercises submitting the Audibertian texts to every conceivable critical approach, from Freudian psychoanalysis to semiotics.

In the. last few years, publishers like Gallimard and Place revived several of the author's old editions which had long been out of print, stimulated by rising new interest in the author's early works, in his poetry and his novels.

In the present study, I have attempted to present a comprehensive but very general introduction to the author's entire production, with an emphasis on the works that are among his best known or most typical. Following an introductory, biographical chapter, I proceed to deal, though perhaps somewhat cursorily, with the author's poetry and narrative prose, in chapters two and three, respectively. Alas, those are areas deserving of more attention. But given my constraints of space, I had no choice but to defer a more thorough treatment to another occasion. Chapters four, five and six deal almost exclusively with the author's drama. My analyses are attempts at thematic accounts of content intended for a direct acquaintance with the dramatist's fictions. Finally, in chapter seven, as well as in the concluding chapter eight, my aim is to assess a measure of the author's originality and the merits of his contributions as a man of letters. It is in these two chapters that I deal with the intricacies of his style and with the implications of the personal philosophical message couched in the texts of his massive production.

For my primary sources, I relied mainly on existing editions, some of which are old and difficult to locate. For documents in limited or special editions, I have benefited from extensive use of the resources of the Bibliothèque Nationale, as well as of those of the Arsenal, in Paris. My quotations from primary, as well as from secondary, sources are almost all in the language of the original document involved (French or English). To this date, none of Audiberti's works have been translated into English, in this or any other country.

I wish to express here my debt and gratitude to a very special group of people without whose advice and help the completion of this book might not have been possible. I owe a special debt to the Friends of Jacques Audiberti, many of whom I met for the first time at Cerisy, during the Audiberti colloquium in 1976. An inestimable amount of biographical information became available to me in the course of the brief, informal discussions I had with them then. I am particularly indebted to Michel Giroud with whom I had several long conversations and extremely constructive exchanges. I am equally indebted to Marie-Louise Audiberti-Ponti, the author's younger daughter, whose generous authorizations afforded me access to otherwise unobtainable documents, and who also read portions of this book and generously communicated to me corrections and suggestions for improvements. Incomparably greater is my debt to Jeanyves Guérin who read the first draft of the book in its entirety and offered me precious advice, and who never failed to assist me in every way possible during my research, both here and in Paris. Finally, I wish to express my deep appreciation to my wife Miriam for her patience in typing the manuscript for this book and for her suggestions and comments on the elaboration of this text.

CONSTANTIN TOLOUDIS

University of Rhode Island

Chronology

1899   March 25. Birth of Jacques-Séraphin-Marie Audiberti, son of Louis Audiberti and of Victorine Médard, in Antibes.

1899– Studies at the Collège d'Antibes. Experiences difficulties in
1917   adjusting to school life.

1918– Employed by the townhall of Antibes as a clerk at the local
1924   courthouse.

1924   Arrival in Paris. Through Emile Condroyer, a former classmate at the College of Antibes, he secures employment with *Le Journal* as a *"tourneur"* in the suburbs.

1925   He joins *Petit Parisien*. Frequents the café Dome at a time when Gaston Bonheur, Camille Bryen, and later, Trotski were among the "regulars" there. Marries a school teacher from the Carribean Islands.

1930   Publishes *L'Empire et la Trappe*, a collection of poems, drawing the attention of Jean de Bosschère and Valéry Larbaud. Jean Cassou reviews the book in *Les Nouvelles Littéraires*.

1933   Meets Jean Paulhan. Has his first contribution published in *NRF*.

1935   Becomes the recipient of the first Prix Mallarmé. The occasion is celebrated by a dinner party which was attended by Paul Valéry, Léon-Paul Fargue, Jean Cocteau, Saint-Pol Roux, Paul Fort, Charles Vildrac, Jean Ajalbert, André Fontainas, Ferdinand Hérold and Edouard Dujardin.

1937   Is awarded the "Prix de la meilleure pièce en un acte," for his *L'Ampelour*. Lives alone in hotels or apartments the addresses of which he tries to keep secret.

1940   Resigns his post as a reporter but continues his association with *Petit Parisien*. Settles in the Hôtel Taranne, where Gaston Bonheur, Marcel Mirouze, Arthur Adamov also reside.

1941– Publishes articles in *Comoedia* on cinema. Meets Jacques
1942   Baratier at the Bibliothèque Nationale. Lives on his penmanship. Takes trips to the Vosges, to Alsatia, Germany, Savoy, southern France, Antibes (which he visits every summer). Writes in cafés, in *Les Deux Magots*, often sitting next to Sartre and Simone de Beauvoir. Meets Jean Duvignaud.

1943   Death of Louis Audiberti, the poet's father.

1946   *Quoat-Quoat*, his first full-length play, is produced at Gaité-Montparnasse, with André Reybaz directing. In *Les Deux Magots*, where he also meets Boris Vian and Juliette Greco, the painter Annenkoff introduces him to Georges Vitaly.

1948   He attends Antonin Artaud's much talked about lecture at the Vieux-Colombier.

1951   Publishes articles in *Cahiers du cinéma*. Travels to Egypt in response to an invitation. Meets Gabriel Bounoure who, in 1938, wrote a favorable review of *Race des hommes* in *NRF*.

1955   Vitaly produces *Le Mal court* in a triumphant comeback at the Théâtre la Bruyère, with settings created by Leonor Fini. His reputation is now established as that of a major playwright of the budding avant-garde of French postwar drama.

1956   Henri Amer, friend of Gabriel Bounoure, publishes "Audiberti, romancier de l'incarnation," first major comprehensive study of Audiberti's novels (*NRF*, Oct.–Nov. 1956).

1962   In one year alone three of his plays are produced on the stage in theater halls of Paris. The press takes notice. Production of *La Fourmi dans le corps* at the Comédie Française where it is hissed and booed by the Tuesday evening devotees of Classical theater.

1964   Is the recipient of the Grand Prix des Lettres and of the Prix des Critiques.

1965   July 10. Dies from an attack of cancer in his Paris apartment where he had just been brought from the hospital following a painful kidney ailment.

CHAPTER 1

A Stranger from Occitania

I *Youth in Antibes*

THERE are few poet-dramatists in the history of contemporary theater whose reputations rest quite so exclusively on the virtually undefinable multiplicity of talent now permanently associated with the name of Jacques Audiberti. Magician, minstrel, philosopher, devotee of the occult, visionary, great lyricist of torrential exuberance, Audiberti the prodigy is at the present time routinely cited by historians of twentieth century theater as one of the most refreshingly original stylists to have appeared since the last war. He is compared with authors as diverse in sensitivity and intellect as Claudel and Céline, Rabelais and Mallarmé, Hugo and Raymond Roussel. He is often referred to as one of the most important proponents of what came to be termed for a time *"Théâtre poétique nouveau,"* or *"Avant-garde poétique"* of the theater and thus placed in a class with Ghelderode, Pichette, Vauthier, Tardieu and Schéhadé.[1] And among the traits of his personal style, his works have been said to display a bewildering mixture of sixteenth century baroque expansiveness, classical formal perfectionism and a dashing, almost irrational irreverence of Surrealist inspiration.

By close friends and mere acquaintances alike, he is unreservedly described with hyperbolic epithets expressing either knowing praise or candid wonderment. Jean de Bosschère, painter and poet, and one of his oldest friends wrote:

C'est un homme corpulent qui donne du mal aux tissages et aux fils de ses habits. Il les use en quelques jours, c'est consumer qu'il faut dire, ou peut-être qu'il les frotte à la lime, les fait bouillir dans une fièvre de gestes et de paroles.[2]

Jean Cassou, art critic and also a long time friend remembering the very first visit the poet paid him, refers to him as "ce robuste garçon à la tête romaine, à la voix chaude, très légèrement voilée"[3] which instantly inspired in him an "irresistible fondness." Leonor Fini, the enchanting painter of quasi-Botticellian elegance and of striking psychoanalytic, Surrealistic and mystical intuitions was also an Audiberti admirer and close friend. Once she wrote:

Les hommes, les objets, les idées et les mots qui désignent les hommes, les objets, les idées sont comme des morceaux de verre dans le kaléidoscope Audibertien. Il suffit qu'il les agite pour que nous voyons la plus belle des étoiles, non seulement la plus belle mais la plus juste.[4]

The poet and novelist André Pieyre de Mandiargues, one of the most attentive and best informed analysts of Audiberti's poetry observed:

Loin au-dessus des autres belles qualités qu'il m'avait permis d'apercevoir, Audiberti, pour moi, était un prodigieux réservoir de mots, si prodigieux qu'il me faut remonter dans le passé jusqu'à l'un des poètes qui ont depuis longtemps ma préférence, le luxuriant Guillaume de Salluste, Seigneur du Bartas, pour trouver quelqu'un qui soit un peu de son espèce.[5]

The sociologist and political theorist Gaston Bouthoul, in a characteristic reference to the time when, toward the end of the war, he would regularly meet with Audiberti in Antibes and carry on unending conversations with him, comments:

Les événements historiques, sources d'enthousiasme pour la plupart des hommes, ne lui causaient qu'étonnement renforcé par sa modestie. Personne mieux que lui ne savait raconter sa stupeur et l'expliquer jusqu'à lui faire partager l'insolite des situations les plus traditionnelles, séculaires et normales.[6]

On a more recent occasion, Eugène Ionesco who has always considered Audiberti a "prestigious writer," makes a similar remark by referring specifically to the dramatist's language:

Ce n'était pas seulement la richesse de son vocabulaire qui me surprenait, mais la justesse des nouveaux rapports qu'il établissait, de façon inattendu, entre des mots, des notions, jusqu'à lui irréconciliables . . . Je le lisais, attentivement, pour découvrir à quel moment la magie jouait, comment il faisait pour arriver à cette couleur, à cette lumière de la phrase, à cette réussite.[7]

And the well known director of the N.R.F. Jean Paulhan, once all powerful arbiter of taste in the world of letters and culture, once made the unequivocal statement: "Je n'irai pas jusqu'à dire qu'Audiberti a inventé le théâtre. Ce n'est pas vrai, le théâtre existait déjà. Mais, de toute évidence, il l'aurait inventé s'il avait fallu."[8]

As for the record of his production, it is of staggering proportions. Audiberti's published works to date include ten collections of poems, some twenty novels, dozens of essays, chronicles, prefaces, adaptations and translations, and an as yet unknown number of articles and book reviews which he published on request in newspapers, magazines and a variety of literary journals. He is also credited with a considerable number of water colors and drawings reflecting some of the obsessions and themes which occur in his written works as well. Above all, he is best known today as the author of twenty-six plays almost all of which have been produced on the stage, at one time or another.

To this date, there is no published, comprehensive biography of Jacques Audiberti. All that is known of his life is based more or less haphazardly: 1) on the author's partly biographical works (cf. *Monorail, Cent jours, Dimanche m'attend, La Nâ et al.*) in which he writes about himself often depicted in slightly fictionalized situations, 2) on accounts of different periods or events of his life which he gave during interviews, or on less formal occasions, 3) on testimonies of friends who knew him intimately and shared important moments either of his childhood and early youth or of his career as a mature writer, and 4) on factual information established through his correspondence which unfortunately is still not completely public.

Jacques Séraphin Audiberti was born in Antibes on March 25, 1899. It is there that he spent his childhood and his adolescence. It is to that small, ancient town on the Mediterranean coast that he often returned later to spend long summer vacations or to meditate. Throughout his life, Audiberti made no secret of the immense attraction he always felt toward this town of contrasts, toward these sites of perpetual enchantment, immersed in the mythical atmosphere as he strolled on the *"Remparts"* or in the streets between them where the echoes and shadows of the remote Languedocian past blend in with the shouts and weird-sounding exclamations of English-speaking tourists who had been invading the area since the turn of the century.

He was born in the house of his paternal grandparents, on rue du Saint-Esprit, in the old section of town, where his parents stayed till he was six. His father who was a mason then decided to build a house of his own, in Anse Saint Roch, the bourgeois section of the town, between the port and the Fort carré. This is the house where Jacques Audiberti lived till he was twenty-four. It is the house from which, in 1924, he left for Paris in search of a new life, and a new home. In a manner very typical of him, he never ceased to remind his friends and his readers that his ties with this house were strong and that more than once, he returned to visit it and reminisce in it even after it had long changed proprietors. Interestingly, his memories from both his early homes were in fact most vivid. In *Monorail* as well as in *Cent jours*, he evokes in precious detail the objects which he associated with his own perception of the Napoleonian legend since childhood, and which were among the first stimuli that gradually shaped his sense of history. In his grandmother's house, he recalled a portrait of Maréchal Victor (probably a reproduction of the popular painting by Gros), and also a picture representing the battle of Austerlitz in which "le duc de Montebello, tous les membres galonnés, conduisait des mameloucks attiffés comme des grillons. L'Empereur était entouré de rayons" (*Monorail*, p. 26).

Aside from Vauban's and Napoleon's respective ghosts with whom he seems to be in constant communion, Audiberti displays an equally intense interest in the "Rocks of Antibes" which incite him to meditate on the preRenaissance, even on the prehistoric life of the town. By innumerable allusions to its various periods, he demonstrates in no uncertain terms how permanently engaged he is in the probing, in the discovery and awareness of mystical, if not improbable, ties with this land and its past. In a chapter of his novel *La Nâ* pointedly entitled "Pierres d'Antibes," he exclaims: "Antipolis[9] . . . Ville contraire . . . Ville de pierre. Ville du Rempart, de Septentrion, du marbre d'Aphrodite, du Port, du Sale, du carré des Tours, [. . .] je suis ton fils" (*La Nâ*, p. 232).

It is worth noting at this juncture that the haunting presence of a huge sculpture representing a head in stone assumes a symbolic significance of the first order in the plot of this novel. And in addition to myths and symbols, Antibes is also the key to understanding Audiberti's first exposure to violence, cruelty, injustice, as Michel Giroud so aptly points out.[10] For it is in those early days of his life that he became aware of the ills and imperfections of mankind which he was to denounce so uncompromisingly in the different stages of his "Abhumanist" thought. As an adolescent at school, he was tormented by his inability to cope with his math teacher as well as by his inability to comprehend the subject. He was suffering even more by his inability to adjust to that environment emotionally. Under the guise of fiction, in a narrative dealing with the same period of his life, he intimates the same type of experiences, in the same vivid detail:

> A la récréation, Damase se vit entouré, brusquement, d'une troupe hurlante de types qui dansaient autour de lui avec une haine grimaçante, en montrant ses genoux qui, comme d'habitude, étaient sales. Les types riaient. Les types dansaient. "Brutapeou! criaient-ils. Crasseuse peau." Allait-il devenir ce gibier que la meute dévore dans la cour des écoles? Les types, la meute dansait. Damase se précipitait vers l'un, vers l'autre. De toute sa terreur, de toute sa tendresse, il s'efforçait de toucher ces visages, de les ouvrir, de leur faire goûter son coeur, ses larmes. Mais les types dansaient toujours. Sans la sonnerie, ils l'auraient tué. (*Monorail*, p. 69)

Any kind of violence, any form of cruelty horrified the young child in those days. It is there, in Antibes, that he lived through the constraints of an authoritarian father "who terrorized the sensitive and timid lad."[11] In *Monorail*, he lets us benefit from many a lively description of the man with "hoarse, bombastic voice," with "royal and voracious majesty," with "black beard," and "shining teeth" known everywhere as a captivating story-teller and practical joker. Particularly interesting is the mocking pastime which dealt with the "last judgment," one of his favorite games, a sort of ritual that was concluded by sentencing the child to a hundred thirty-eight years in purgatory, and his wife to hell, while the maid was granted the ultimate of rewards and sent to paradise. Understandably, both the child and the mother dreaded the game.

It is also here in Antibes that Audiberti's timidity toward women became apparent when he had his first experience of desire and thereby acquired his first fears of lust. It is here that we can trace the ingredients and understand the triggering mechanisms of his erotic obsessions which so dominated the thematic content of his works later. Analyzing that phase of his life in retrospect, again in *La Nâ*, he wrote:

> Juan-les-Pins, quartier d'Antibes. [. . .] Toi, le don Juan de la romance espagnole, nauffragé sur le paradis de cette côte, tu désignes par ton prénom la plage où l'homme et la femme, depuis mil neuf cent treize et furieusement à partir de mil neuf cent vingt, mêlèrent leurs jambes dans la mer translucide, se mouillèrent ensemble à l'humeur du plaisir déployée et miroitante au-delà de l'horizon, et puisèrent dans le breuvage d'épiderme la jeunesse. . . . et moi, dans mon noir pardessus, les mains sur l'angoisse du coeur, au mois de juillet, à vingt ans, la bouche dans le foulard, j'avais peur d'aller dans le bain. Je n'étais pourtant que désir . . . (*La Nâ*, p. 230)

It is finally also in Antibes that Audiberti's cataclysmic lyricism became, in the Audibertian poetic vision, fixed in its basic tone, imagery and prosodic patterns. Abundant evidence that this is so can be found on practically every page of every one of his works. Perhaps the most characteristic of his own assessments in this respect would be a statement he made in a seminal, immensely revealing moment of reflexion:

> . . . je me souviens de m'être, un jour, laissé tomber devant une ville, comme saisi dans l'épaisseur d'un coup de foudre de lumière, en criant que c'était trop beau. Treize ans, j'avais, je me souviens aussi d'avoir, un autre jour, dévalé la Garoupe en clamant, pour la seul fois de ma vie, des mots que me dictaient les pins, les rochers calcinés, les éclats de mer bleue au bout des chemins rouges. Mon printemps chantait les dieux grecs dont jamais, plus tard, je ne parlai, et ce lyrisme bondissant, de toute manière non recueilli, ce péan éparpillé aux arbres nerveux et aux ossements du roc ébréché, rassemblés à composer l'immortelle dureté du marbre méditerranéen aux estompes de saphir, il fut sans doute le plus fervent, le seul valable des hymnes que j'aurai tentés.[11]

At the close of his secondary education in 1915, his future in Antibes seems far from promising. His first employment following graduation in all probability was less than exciting to him: He was a clerk at the local courthouse. It is very unlikely that during this period he kept up with the latest developments in the world of culture and literature. In an article he wrote considerably later, he intimated that the literary works he read as an adolescent were not what one might call eye openers and by no means representative of any avant-garde: books by Pierre Benoit, Pierre Loti, Henri de Regnier, Anatole France. And while he was already spellbound by Victor Hugo, the author he never ceased to consider unsurpassed and a model to emulate, his dislike, on the other hand, for Apollinaire must also have prevented him from becoming sensitized either to the manifestations of budding Surrealism or to any other signals from the international avant-garde set, as Michel Giroud points out.[12] It is worth noting nevertheless that he did manage to contribute articles rather regularly to *Reveil d'Antibes*, a local weekly of limited means whose publica-tion was terminated in 1923. Significantly enough, in 1914 Audi-berti submitted his first collection of poems to Edmond Rostand who, reportedly, wrote him a very encouraging letter and sent him an autographed photograph. But the author of *L'Aiglon*, still popular with provincial French youth at the time, was to die in 1918 and

Audiberti's life was about to enter into a new phase. In 1924, he was leaving his native Antibes for the exciting national capital where his star was destined to rise.

II   *Apprenticeship in Paris*

As long as almost twenty years after that fateful arrival in Paris, Audiberti continued to attach an enormous significance to the emotional and formative role of Antibes as a setting of his real origins. In *La Nâ* he wrote:

> Ma vie, ma barque, a deux pôles, Antibes, Paris. Antibes m'offre, dans un univers de pierres, l'inguérissable faim de l'homme strictement défini par le vieil ordre catholique et juridique sous la danse funèbre de Septentrion. A Paris je retrouve la pierre des pierres, la sainte Pierre, la négative, la convexe ou toutes les flèches se brisent et qui congèle le pain de l'âme. (*La Nâ*, p. 233)

Once he even made the claim that "the beauties of his province and native town were veiled to him by the fascination of 'printed matter' coming from Paris."[13] Yet it is rather obvious that he ended up yielding to the temptation. Audiberti the writer was formed mainly in Paris. His first mentor was Emile Condroyer. It is under his influence and patronage that Audiberti joined the *Journal* and later the *Petit parisien:* "Je suis venu à Paris, en principe pour y rejoindre Emile Condroyer, que j'avais connu au collège d'Antibes, qui fut l'un des parrains de la littérature de reportage pittoresque qui par la suite, prit en France une grande extension. C'était aussi un parfait poète."[14]

The profession he embarked upon at that time he liked to refer to, not without a hint of tenderness, as *"tourneur."* The function of a *tourneur* consists in making the rounds, day after day, of a sizable number of police precincts for the purpose of gathering information on small news items from the records of the day's events. For a period of five years, as a reporter-scavenger roaming the ghettoes and the less fashionable suburbs, he received an extensive education in the poetry of marginal life in some of the most unglamorous sections of Paris (Bagnolet, Place Gambetta, Père Lachaise, Port Saint-Denis). The themes varied very little from day to day: fires, muggings, kidnappings, rapes, suicides, murders and the like. Burning with the fever of poetry, he managed to find time to write, even during this hectic period of his life. In the course of his first stay in Paris, his acquaintances were still among the unknown or marginal of the literary crowd that was conspicuous in the capital of the *Belle époque.*

Things were to change somewhat when he met Benjamin Péret, through whom he became aware of the ambitions of the ongoing Surrealist revolution and by whom he was initiated into knowledge of Picasso's painting. Benjamin Péret, already privileged sacristan in Breton's chapel, was nonetheless a *tourneur* like Audiberti. The latter always took pains to clarify that he never became a full-fledged member of the Surrealist club: "Je ne suis pas entré dans le groupe. Ce n'était pas mon chemin. Je n'avais rien à leur apporter," he explained to Paul Guth during an interview.[15] But Péret did try to endoctrinate him and spoke to him regularly of Breton whom Audiberti was to meet in person later. There is even evidence that Audiberti may have read at least some of Breton's books. Shortly afterward, he severed his ties with *Journal* to join the staff of the *Petit parisien* where he met André Salmon, another great journalist and poet. Reflecting on his professional status and on his state of mind in those days, he wrote, "Ambitieux, certes je l'étais, l'étant depuis ma naissance et de plus loin sans doute encore, mais, en même temps, incapable de démarches, d'initiative, de la moindre invention active et précise" (*Cent jours*, p. 253).

In 1926, he married a young school teacher from the Carribean Islands. She was, in the words of Gaston Bonheur, "belle comme une idole en bois de teck, et créole comme Joséphine." And in keeping with an old habit of his, he used to refer to her as "la pierre" or the "Croix d'ambre."[16] Then in 1930 he published *L'Empire et la Trappe*, his first collection of poems. Though the original edition of this book could only materialize at the author's expense, it elicited an enthusiastic response from Valery Larbaud and earned Audiberti the admiration of Jean de Bosschère. Jean Cassou who, at the time, used to write the column on poetry in *Nouvelles littéraires*, analyzed the collection in a brief review, the first study ever to be published on Audiberti.

The life of the *tourneur* from Antibes seemed to be taking a new turn. Several well known reviews now solicit contributions from him. Soon his acquaintances would include Fombeure, Ivan and Claire Goll, Paulhan, Léon-Paul Fargue. In the period from 1930 to about 1934 he composed a large number of poems many of which were to appear later in *La Pluie sur les boulevards*, published in 1950. In 1935 he became the first recipient of the Prix Mallarmé which had just been instituted, and whose first panel of judges was formed of Paul Valéry, Jean Cocteau, Léon-Paul Fargue, Gérard d'Houville, Charles Vildrac, Ferdinand Hérold, André Fontainas, Edouard Dujardin and Jean Ajalbert. By 1934, he had met personally Drieu la

Rochelle, with whom he became friends, André Malraux whom he always considered the greatest novelist of the twentieth century, Louis Aragon, and Jean Cocteau. In 1937 his play *L'Ampelour* won the "Prix de la meilleure pièce en un acte." In Ville d'Avray, in a villa owned by Henry and Barbara Church, American patrons of the arts, he met most of the writers of the N.R.F. Close ties with the N.R.F. were assiduously sought after in those days by writers whose credentials were less than universally recognized. In *Dimanche m'attend* Audiberti still remembers how fortunate he was to enjoy an early association with the fabulous institution which he rates as "obligatoire école polytechnique et première communion solonnelle de l'écrivain" (p. 29). It is about this time that he got involved in the activities of a group publishing a review, *Le Beau navire*, and started collaborating with, among others, Luc Estang, Maurice Fombeure, and Maurice Chapelan, the chief editor. As a journalist, he was now promoted to reporter (1935). His work for the paper was no longer anonymous. He was given assignments requiring extensive travel. But when he was in Paris he spent most of his time reading in the Bibliothèque Nationale. In 1937 he had a meeting with Paulhan who spoke to him about *Abraxas*, Audiberti's first novel, his most ambitious one, which was to appear the following year. Also in 1937 he published his second collection of poems, *Race des hommes*, in which he reveals himself to be "metallurgiste du vers," "burineur des solides," "mielleur de language ouvragé dans la tradition de Valéry."[17]

During the war and shortly afterward, he lived mostly in Paris, even after 1950, when he acquired his own house in Lozère. In 1940 he resigned his post with the *Petit parisien* presumably to have more freedom and time to devote to creative writing. The hotel Taranne, on Boulevard Saint-Germain, was now his residence where he lived as a bachelor (he had been living mostly alone since 1937). The setting in this hotel will be evoked in interesting detail later in *Talent*, one of his autobiographical novels, published in 1947, in which Taranne appears under the fictional name of Pompelane. Under financial pressure, however, he felt he had little choice but to write reviews (of films, plays and books) for *Comoedia* and *Aujourd'hui*, in order to gain the advantage of immediate remuneration. He also published poems in reviews such as *Poésie 42, Fontaine, Confluences*, and *Pyrénées*. He now was participating in the social life of the sixteenth Arrondissement. Here he met, among others, Ludmilla Vlasto with whom he entered into what turned out to be a life-long friendship. This relationship was not without certain practical advantages later,

once Ludmilla Vlasto founded the Théâtre la Bruyère where several
of Audiberti's plays were produced.
    He had to flee from Paris in 1940. His stay in the backwoods of the
Massif Central is described with little disguise in his novel *Urujac*.
But the escape from the capital was only temporary. He returned to
Paris the same year. As Michel Giroud points out, the period
1940–1947 may well be the most fertile period of Audiberti's entire
life. His writing was then dominated by his all-pervasive preoccupation with *"Abhumanisme,"* his one and only attempt to formulate a
coherent system or philosophy of his personal brand (an attempt
which remained rather blatantly unsuccessful). This is the period of
La Nouvelle origine, intended as a manifesto launching a bi-monthly
review, under a project that never materialized, and which marks
perhaps the beginning of the author's serious reflexion on Abhumanism. It is in this period that he busily published articles in *L'Age
d'or, Le Spectateur, Opéra, La Table ronde*, and narratives like *Le
Victorieux* (1947), *Le Retour du Divin* (1943) and *Carnage* (1942), a
novel that can easily be rated the best piece of prose fiction he ever
wrote. This is also the period of translations of and prefaces to,
Joppolo's novels. Toward the end of the war, when he returned to
Antibes for another short stay, he met regularly with a group of
writers who had sought refuge there from the yet unliberated parts of
the country (Aragon, Auric, Cocteau, Eluard, Emmanuel, Claude
Roy and Pierre Seghers among others). Here he already displayed his
henceforth legendary inability to settle down in one residence for any
normal length of time. In his native town, he no longer owned the
house on rue du Saint-Esprit. When he returned to these parts for a
visit, he stayed with friends or relatives but was uncomfortable
everywhere. As it has often been observed by those who knew
Audiberti well, "il ne put jamais habiter vraiment ni son corps, ni ses
chaussures, ni ses maisons, ni les nombreux appartments qu'il
connaître après la guerre."[18]

III   *A Dramatist's Search for Recognition*

    If the period 1940–47 was the most fertile, the one immediately
following and extending up to the last day of his life in that sad
summer of 1965 is definitely the most gratifying, the most rewarding
and, in many ways, one might say simply, the happiest for the poet
from Antibes. Not that his art as a writer is at this point marked by
any extraordinary rises in his status, enhancing his prestige. Strange
as it may seem, it would be a misleading exaggeration even to suggest

that Audiberti's style of language or composition changed at any time during his entire life in any significant way. If his two last collections of verse, *Lagune hérissée* (1958) and *Ange aux entrailles* (1964) display indeed what Michel Giroud calls "a harsh, raucous tone of popular ballad," and if his novels tend to favor a manner of "popular narrative" heavily spiced with argot and with the "vivid language of the streets," very little in this apparent modification is indicative of any manner of inventiveness and enrichment, either in the thematic content or in the literary devices manifest in his texts. But one significant change did occur. In a change of tactics rather than substance, Audiberti became more and more persistently driven to attempt another format. His creativeness, becoming redirected gradually, turned toward theatrical production. It was a shift that enlarged his audience so drastically and so rapidly that to this date, more than a decade after his death, he is still best known principally as a dramatist.

His career in the theater began almost accidentally. In 1946 André Reybaz and Catherine Toth decided to take the risks of a first attempt by producing *Quoat-Quoat* at the Gaité-Montparnasse. The venture was incredibly daring not only because Audiberti was unknown as a dramatist, but also because of a rather prohibitive lack of material means. Then that same year Audiberti had the good fortune to meet Georges Vitaly, then an aspiring young director with a sense of commitment and already working on his serious plans to create a "Shock Theater" on the Left Bank.[19] The following year, Vitaly directed a production of *Le Mal court*, the dramatist's best known play, at the Théâtre de Poche. The audience was minute and the event was hardly noticed at the time. Ironically, this same director's staging of a triumphantly successful revival of the same play at the Théâtre la Bruyère in 1955 is perhaps the one single event that provided the decisive push for the launching of Audiberti as a dramatist to be reckoned with. He first scored a few half-successes and a few *"Succès de scandale."* With a few exceptions (notably that of Jacques Lemarchand in *Combat*), the drama critics of the press resisted him rather consistently, at first. But gradually his plays were to be seen performed in larger theaters, including the Comédie Française where a noisy debut of his *La Fourmi dans le corps* in 1962 had been viewed by some critics as reminiscent of the epoch-making *"bataille d'Hernani"* occasioned by the stormy performance of Victor Hugo's play in this bastion of conservatism, in 1830.

That same year, Audiberti's name figured equally prominently in numerous articles and reviews by the daily press in connection with

La Poupée, one of his novels which had been made into a film by Jacques Baratier. Needless to say, by this time, twelve years after his death, his works had been played not only in Paris and all over France but also in other countries, notably in Germany, Belgium, the Netherlands and in the United States. In 1948 Vitaly produced a second Audiberti play at the Théâtre de la Huchette. This time he chose *La Fête noire* which is perhaps the most technically polished of Audiberti's dramas. And from then on he seems to find the products of the Audiberti factory rather difficult to resist.

As has been the case with many a playwright before, a series of theatrical successes is credited as much to the director as to the author. Indeed we can safely say that in the beginnings of what was shaping as Audiberti's theater there was definitely a phase dominated by Vitaly's directorship. A distinct type of stage show came into being by virtue of the particular approach and personal touch adopted for the Audibertian texts by the group that subsequently became the Compagnie Georges Vitaly. For a number of years, the group's repertory featured Audiberti plays so regularly that it appeared that the choices were dictated by contractual commitments. The explanation no doubt is that from 1953 onward Audiberti wrote plays with particular actors and directors in mind, as Jeanyves Guérin points out. Clearly then, Vitaly represents a major influence in the playwright's evolution in this direction. First at the Théâtre de la Huchette and later at the Théâtre la Bruyère, his initiatives would continue to create theatrical events with *Pucelle* (1950), *Les Naturels du Bordelais* (1953), and following the revival of *Le Mal court*, with *Le Ouallou* (1957), *L'Effet Glapion* (1959), and *Pomme, Pomme, Pomme* (1962).

Other directors also have during this period occasionally produced Audiberti plays—but without leaving personal imprints. Aside from the courageous and talented André Reybaz who directed *Quoat-Quoat* and *L'Ampelour*, Jean le Poulain produced and presented *La Hobereaute* once at the IVe Festival des Nuits de Bourgogne, in 1956, and again at the Théâtre du Vieux Colombier, in 1958. And the year André Barsacq produced *La Fourmi dans le corps* (1962) at the Comédie Française, Françoise Spira was launching another venture with *La Brigitta*, at the Athenée, with very little success to be sure. The only other director whose impact might be viewed as comparable to Vitaly's is perhaps Marcel Maréchal whose exemplary production of *Le Cavalier seul* at the Théâtre du Cothurne in Lyon, in 1963, represents no doubt the second crucial event in Audiberti's evolution in the theater, opening for him the way to the prestigious and well-publicized summer festivals (Festival du Marais, Festival d'Avignon and the like). Through the Maréchal approach, Audiberti became integrated with the best theatrical traditions of the Elilzabethan and of the French Baroque eras, as Jeanyves Guérin has demonstrated in his study of the Baroque in Audiberti's theater. Interestingly, in his assessment of these new fortunes of the dramatist's works, Jeanyves Guérin also seems to believe that Maréchal's vision and directorial skills attained the ultimate in exploiting the intrinsic theatricality of Audiberti's plays.[20]

Jacques Audiberti the playwright achieved almost overnight what he could not accomplish as a poet or as a novelist for years. With the clear projection of his public image as a dramatist he became a celebrity. In 1948 he received the Charles-Veillon award. He then began writing articles for the well known weekly *Arts* while he continued to send contributions to *La Nouvelle N.R.F., La Parisienne* and *Cahiers du cinéma.* In 1954 he was a serious contestant for the Prix des Critiques. The judges were confronted this time with a choice between Audiberti's *Les Jardins et les fleuves* and Sagan's *Bonjour Tristesse.* As it is known, the prize was awarded to the latter, perhaps somewhat unfairly, at least so thought some critics who, outraged at the verdict at the time, made their voices heard. Audiberti had the satisfaction of receiving the same prize ten years later, in 1964, the year he also received the Grand Prix des Lettres, which in his case was decided upon by unanimous vote. Following the publication of his *Molière* in 1954 he became acquainted with Gaston Bachelard. The latter had commented—as Jean-Paul Sartre and Brice Parain had done before—on the much talked-about Audibertian image of the "secret blackness of milk," in *La Terre et les rêveries du repos* (1948), before he had read anything else by Audiberti. To let Audiberti know of his enthusiasm, this time Bachelard wrote him a letter:

Je vous lis. Quand ma langue s'emparesse j'ouvre *La Pluie sur les boulevards* et le monde se remet à tourner . . . Mais nous sommes faits pour nous comprendre. Avec vous, à 71 ans, j'ai l'impression de réapprendre ma langue maternelle [. . .][21]

He was suddenly much interviewed on radio and in newspapers during trips he took in France and abroad. Responding to an invitation, in 1955 Audiberti visited Egypt where he met Gabriel

Bounoure in person. Bounoure, long an admirer of his, in 1938 had published a eulogistic review of *Race des hommes* in *N.R.F.* At various times, Audiberti also traveled to Belgium, Germany and Italy. In 1956 and again in 1959, his articles in *Arts* reveal him as anguished over the status of poets and poetry. In July, 1962, having read the celebrated structural analysis of Baudelaire's "Les Chats" by Jakobson and Lévi-Strauss, Audiberti wrote to the latter (with whom he had been corresponding probably since 1960 and whose work he was reading with a great deal of interest):

> Après de tels poèmes est-il utile de continuer à faire des vers? Mon inquiétude concerne volontiers la vanité des réalités. Peut-être avez-vous feuilleté quelque recueil de moi, prosodique et rimé? Gallimard me demande d'en publier de nouveau. Mais à quoi bon? Le "quorum," à travers Baudelaire, Hugo, Leconte de Lisle, n'est-il pas atteint des oeuvres scansibles et memorables qui manquaient à l'univers?[22]

Two years later, in 1964, he did publish a new collection of verse all the same and with Gallimard as his publisher: *Ange aux entrailles*. It was his last lyrical outburst, fashioned with the same dosage of bitterness covered by humor or buffoonery that we find in his previous collections, mixed with what Michel Giroud describes as, "la grande pitié d'un homme qui ne veut pas pleurer lâchement."[23] In 1963 and 1964 appeared in *N.R.F. La Guérite* and *La Guillotine*, short plays evoking Robespierre and the atmosphere of the period, in the usual Audibertian manner. In 1964 his health deteriorated rapidly. One of the friends closest to him at the time reports that he withstood the sickness of his last year with almost quiet resignation:

> Cette année de maladie, pour d'autres un cauchemar, il l'a supportée pres-que heureux de ne plus bouger de son gite, de consacrer ses forces, non plus à traverser les rues, entre les voitures, à trouver un restaurant, à traîner aux *Deux-Magots*, à chercher un appartement, mais à écrire, écrire, écrire, sa raison de vivre.[24]

In 1965, less than a month before his death Gallimard published *Dimanche m'attend*, Audiberti's last autobiographical narrative, bringing to a close at once his career as a writer and his anguish-ridden life. When he completed the final draft of his manuscript he was moving in and out of the subdued light of surgery clinics. Could he have been at least partly conscious of the impending end? There are no clear indications in the text of the book. And yet the title seems to have been coined with a frightful premonition. Jacques Séraphin Audiberti expired during the night of Saturday, July 10, 1965.

To honor his memory, the town council of Antibes named one of the town squares Place Audiberti. Also, the school that nurtured the poet's childhood and teens, the college of Antibes that the author of *Monorail* evoked so vividly, is now called Lycée Audiberti.

CHAPTER 2

The Empire and the Retreat

I *Thematic Variations*

IF the first signs of Audiberti's literary destiny were collections of poems, and if he first attracted attention to his name by *L'Empire et la Trappe* and later by *Race des Hommes*, his ten major books of verse published during his lifetime are little known and even less read today. Yet it is an undisputed fact that, by temperament as much as by conscious design, Audiberti has always been a poet, in every sense of that word. For it is obvious in every type of text he wrote that beyond a distinct predilection for diffuse, proliferating imagery, his use of his medium is consistently marked by an irresistible desire to explore and exploit the "physical" properties of language. Indeed, he often privileges rhythm, rhyme and every other type of auditory effect or phonetic value to the extent of restating the old, thorny problems arising from the norms and deviations of poetic language as related to the fundamental laws of signification. This is clearly the case as much in *L'Empire et la Trappe* which corresponds to his very first effort, as in *Ange aux entrailles*, his last collection of poems, published one year before he died.

But it is also the case in his other works as well, whether they appeared as drama or narrative prose. In almost every play or novel, this tendency constantly becomes apparent in inventions of plot structures and fiction modeled to accommodate insertions of poems or songs. By its very texture, the language in both theater and the novel conforms much more with the economy of poetic discourse than it does with the laws of prose. Characteristically, Etiemble once observed that Audiberti could well present the totality of his works under the rubriques of Poetry of Novel, Poetry of Theater, Poetry of Criticism by much the same reason as Cocteau.[1]

The thematic content of Audiberti's books of verse appears hopelessly diffuse, lacking coherence and unity. The overwhelming

26

feeling we first have is that this massive production of poetic texts came into being in a continuous, unchecked flow to express nothing but chaos and anarchy, a state which is indistinguishable from an incurable lack of discipline in the poetic process. Yet, on a slightly different level, one discerns the immutable nature of a fundamental dualism pervading the world of the poet's imagination and acting almost like an organizing principle. It is an ethical dualism. It fuels a rigorous dialectic. It guides the creative process so as to subordinate all text-generating mechanisms to a few basic polarities.

The single one of these polarities which figures most prominently almost everywhere is already visible in *L'Empire et la Trappe*. In the ten poems of this book, the author is trying "to sketch" what he considers to be the "fundamental religion" of French men of letters who adhere to the idea of "coexistence of a Nietzchean conception of the universe and of a certain mysticism."[2] More than once, Audiberti has also explained that illustrating this polarity discursively in texts elaborated for better consumption and by a wider readership was not his goal, but that nonetheless "the imbrication of these two pre-ponderant tendencies in the world" set the general tone of his book. Indeed in the dense, hermetic, almost inscrutable texts of these poems, recur the most heterogeneous, unexpectedly juxtaposed historical instances chosen to state the variations of this polarity: Greek and Roman myths, Napoleon and his epic era, contemporary France, contemporary Paris and Antibes in their epic dimensions, emerging from a past half real, half fictional . . . and the ethical polarity suggested by "the secret blackness of milk."

In the subsequent volumes of verse, the themes of the expanded consciousness of the author of *L'Empire et la Trappe* who is thirty years old, will vary a bit superficially but will change little in substance. *Race des Hommes*, seven years later, is, as a sensitive and enlightened reader of Audibertian verse pointed out, clearly indicative of growth but without major changes: ". . . pas très différent de *L'Empire et la Trappe*, sinon que pour le fond, la ration de Napoléon, tout de même, est plus supportable, et que pour la forme le langage a gagné encore en aisance, en impulsion et en vivacité . . ."[3] Here too, the thematic content is secondary to form, just as much as in the first collection.

La rime et le rythme de l'alexandrin régulier, à ce régime abondant et furieusement rapide, conduisent à une soumission de la pensée consciente aux mots qui par des voix tout opposées rejoint étrangement l'écriture automatique pratiquée si bien à la même époque par un grand ami d'Audiberti, le surréaliste Benjamin Péret.[4]

The same reaction is reflected in the expert appraisal of Gabriel Bounoure. The latter has nothing but enthusiasm for these "Odes à la terre et à la matière":

> Coulées épaisses et torrentielles, les poèmes de la *Race des Hommes* entraînent un flot d'éclatantes métonymies, imitation ou parodie de l'élan vital ou du rut créateur. Les mots se pressent en rangs serrés ou montent les uns par-dessus les autres, lancés vers des significations qu'ils n'atteindront peut-être pas, *car les noms les plus vrais, vierges d'empressements / Demeurent suspendus derrière les horloges* . . .[5]

In the same article, Gabriel Bounoure goes on to suggest that the essential fiction that haunts Audiberti is no less than the creation of the world or, at least, "Noah's census." He concludes: ". . . je le situe à mi-chemin entre Lucrèce et Giorgio de Chirico, matérialiste épique comme le premier, et comme le second, décorateur en proie au démon du sangrenu grandiose et des baroqueries délirantes."[6]

Following *L'Empire et la Trappe*, Audiberti composed *La Pluie sur les boulevards*, which was to be published nevertheless after *Race des hommes*, in 1950, with a lengthy preface intended as a major manifesto on Audibertian poetics. The themes we distinguish here also defy analysis, just as much as in the first two volumes, in stunning contradiction to assurances given in the preface, as to the "irreproachable clarity" of the title. According to this preface, what the book is about may seem almost too simple: "Il s'agit de l'intime soliloque, au bruit de la pluie, d'un théope tout empâté de glandes et de soifs dans une humanité qui l'atteint mais sur quoi il ne parvient pas à peser" (*Poésies*, p. 31). Audiberti sees himself in the role of a *trouvère* who sings his love to the planet Earth. His procedure is a "parade of Alexandrine verse," except for one sprightlier, livelier piece, composed of "strophes de six, chaque troisième et sixième vers plus brefs que les quatre autres vers, où je supplie les hommes dont je suis l'oeil, de ne pas encore me quitter, tandis qu'en douce virant de bord j'opte pour Venus, pour la vie inconditionnée extravasée, l'anémone, la mer, l'omnitude, l'Abhumanité" (*Poésies*, p. 36).

No theme imaginable is left untouched by this verbal deluge. The thematic counterpoint is also constant, relentless:

> Hors du mystique endroit qui, de nouveau, m'attire
> comme le trou musqué des chèvres le satyre
> Dieu, suprême péché, consterne le héros.
> . . . .

J'ai soif. Il pleut. J'ai soif. Sans cesse. Je ne puis
rien contre, en moi, le sel de la dame des puis.
Aux cafés je pénètre et la bière clapote
de ma bouche servile à mon boyau despote [. . .] (*Poésies*, p. 70)

An emotional state peculiar to the war period is reflected in *Des Tonnes de semence*. Here worlds appear to form "from the very heart of chaos," as M. Chapelan put it.[7] It is a long sequence of hymns, "poèmes de contexture classique consacrés à la dignité de la vocation d'homme,"[8] according to André Deslandes. In an article of the same year, Alain Bosquet observed, "Aux heures graves où paraît *Des Tonnes de semence*, en 1941, il faut se limiter à l'essentiel. Frapper au but, oublier le luxe des débauches lyriques . . ."[9] There are twenty-eight poems in this volume, apparently organized in four groups, but as far as thematic content is concerned nothing could be more diverse or more casually put together. Religious and biblical references abound here also as do such ambitious theological statements as the following:

Adam veut le péché pour lui, pour sa sémence.
Dieu répond par la grâce où l'absoute commence.
Sache, [. . .]
Que Dieu n'a pas fermé l'asile de ses bras [. . .] (*Poésies*, p. 153)

The dualism inaugurated in *L'Empire et la Trappe* does not seem to disappear in this volume either. Its pervasive presence can be discerned in every thematic development:

L'univers' ai-je dit quand je naquis . . . Le signe
ainsi vous m'accordiez, du monstre qui m'attend.
Suis-je encore votre fils, et celui de Satan,
quand j'acquiers les états de la loutre et du cygne
. . . .
Ouragan libérateur! pourquoi m'avoir jeté
hors du jardin, hors du bonheur, vers le vacarme, [. . .]
Je veux tuer ma vie et cesser de mourir. (*Poésies*, pp. 99–103)

It is in this volume also that we find "Latvia," a relatively longer poem, inaugurating a thematic sequence which will, in the works to follow, become a central argument, most likely prefiguring already, as Jeanyves Guérin suggested recently, the gestation of the author's Abhumanist thesis: The speculation that there is no possible exit from the quagmire of human reality, which is by nature impregnated with Evil, other than the mind boggling deflagration of a "cosmic cataclysm," and the destruction of matter and flesh.[10]

Even more diffuse and unfocused are the thematic variations we find in *Toujours*. In this volume of 1943, the poetic vision of the author of *L'Empire et la Trappe* remains attached to the polarities specified in 1930 and thus is basically unaltered. Here we find the long, uneven stanzas of "La Mer," in which the premises of the same pessimism, as Michel Giroud so aptly has pointed out, are once more forcefully restated: ". . . 'La Mer' expose l'ambivalence fondamentale de notre condition, le double sens de chaque signe, tel que, déjà, Baudelaire dans *les Fleurs du Mal* en avait montré l'inextricable réseau."[11]

It is also in *Toujours* that we find the much commented on poem "Stèle aux mots," which represents another revealing *"art poétique,"* a manifesto dealing with the poet's attitude toward his "material," these fascinating objects—words:

> L'ultime, ultime son, écoutez-le! Les seigles,
> plumage d'aigle sans le sang, périmeront.
> . . . .
> Les mots, chaussés de plomb sournois, l'ongle buté,
> jumelés d'isthme entre leurs coups pleins de carottes,
> avec des scions à la pointure des marottes
> je les chéris cessant de nous déconcerter. (*Poésies*, pp. 197–98)

Noticeably more tame and free of bitterness, irony or sarcasm are the twenty-seven poems of *Vive guitare* (1946). Songs, lullabies and other short, often epigram-like pieces intermingle with more serious, more formal ones dealing with the familiar subjects of the Audibertian repertoire (cf. "Chanson," "Berceuse," "Trois mats," "Origine des Empires," "Jacqueline," "Deltas"). As for *Rempart*, the poet's ties with his most favorable source of inspiration, his native Antibes, once more in this thin volume prove to be alivé and radiant. To quote Alain Bosquet again, "*Rempart*, en 1953, chante les retrouvailles avec le soleil, l'azur méditerranéen, Antibes, les plaisirs de bavarder avec soi-même et de faire une belote avec le Seigneur. [. . .] le démon de la sainteté est oublié, et rien ne presse. Il fait bon de ne pas songer à la mort."[12] The rampart is none other than the complex of the old and the new fortifications unmistakably evoking the era of Vauban and the town's remote past. On the other hand, *Lagune hérissée* is dominated by Audiberti's preoccupations with the realistic expectations of a technological era, for the future of the human race (cf.

science-fiction-like adventure over the lagoon of Venice). Carzou's original lithographs of impressive representations complementing the text incontestably provide a precious, added dimension.
In his last collection of verse, *Ange aux entrailles*, Audiberti returns to buffoonery, sarcasm and irony. But the subjects he deals with will not even give the appearance of deviating from his known repertoire: Religion, the tragic dualism in man-flesh and spirit, implications of the messianic promise in the Bible:

A travers le grand être aux volantes vertèbres
Dieu devient cette forme à qui l'on fait la cour.
Il prouve ainsi l'amour qu'il nourrit pour l'amour
jusque dans notre lac de peur et de ténèbres. (*Ange aux entrailles*, p. 28)

Consistent with almost every other book of verse, *Ange aux entrailles* also includes a series of reflections on the literary process, with the creative process fulfilling itself through language (cf. poems on Hugo, Baudelaire, Racine, Aragon, Fargue). There is a good deal of evidence that Audiberti may have given in to pressure from friends and mentors like Jean Paulhan, and actually brought himself to composing verse with more concern for clarity and direct intelligibility.[13] Also, as Jeanyves Guérin observes, Mallarmé's shadow dissipates,[14] the tortured hermeticism of the first poems gives way to pieces of a more popular make-up and inspiration:

Ne sèche pas, chanson! . . . De toi seule s'élance
au-delà de l'été
l'immodéré rameau qui suspend le silence
de la totalité. (*Ange aux entrailles*)

This is a view that seems to be shared by Michel Giroud as well. The latter writes: "Le dernier recueil révèle un poète en pleine puissance qui ne se répète pas, plus simple et plus dense, sans l'éloquence abondante des premiers recueils."[15]

II *Tools and Techniques of a Versemaker*

From *L'Empire et la Trappe* to *Ange aux entrailles*, including all verse he casually inserts into his texts of narrative prose and drama, Audiberti is almost exclusively absorbed by his passion for the phonetic resources of language and the sorcery of meter and rhythm. His unperturbed, almost stubborn concentration on these "primary

effects" which he sees as the essence of poetry and its exclusive
domain, his apparent neglect of meaning and content in favor of
form, explain perhaps why so few comprehensive critical studies have
been attempted, as of this date, on his art of verse-making. The task is
overwhelming, the results ambivalent.

The author's published works include a sizeable amount of texts
which display a persistent, sincere desire to formulate a set of
theoretical premises on the nature of poetry and on the function of
poets: *La Nouvelle origine* (1942), *L'Ouvre-boîte* (1952), the preface
to *La Pluie sur les boulevards* (1950) and to a lesser extent *Molière*
(1954) and *L'Abhumanisme* (1955). Understandably, the effectiveness of these "exposés" is quite limited. Not so much because poetry is
elusive or a "very naïve confession of inadequacy," as he once wrote
(*Les Médecins ne sont pas des plombiers*, p. 34). It is rather because,
unlike Mallarmé, this *"troubadour naturalisé,"*[16] as Georges Perros
calls him, has always been inept in trying to enunciate abstractions.
Significantly, his awareness of the condition of the poet in modern
society is otherwise far from lacking lucidity.

In *La Nouvelle origine*, he proclaims: "Le poète . . . s'autorise de
l'existence d'une langue historique et traditionnelle, qu'il doit ac-
croître, prolonger et, cependant, destituer, pervertir, corrompre"
(p. 56). "Il veut élargir le lexique," writes Michel Giroud, "mais d'autre
part il se cantonne dans les formes strictes de la strophe codifiée dès
le XIIe siècle par les troubadours."[17] The poets he admires most are
Hugo, Leconte de Lisle, Mallarmé, Baudelaire. Surprisingly, while
he can choose to practice the rhyme and meter prescribed by
Malherbe, he can also, in the same text, use argot or the popular
language or images borrowed from clichés of Surrealistic extraction.
His thematic repertoire is conditioned by trivial or perennial
fixations: Suffering, anxiety, death, women, evil, the limitations of
the flesh, God. But it can also deal with issues that reflect the outer
limits of modern thought (cf. "Latvia," *Lagune hérissée, L'Opéra du
monde, La Fin du monde*).

It is more than a mere coincidence that the poets who awarded
Audiberti the Prix Mallarmé in 1934 were predominantly diehards of
the Symbolist school, on a literary scene already overtaken by the
Surrealist storm.

Audiberti, the poet of the 1920's and of the 1930's, felt at home
mostly with the writers of Fargue's generation. His conception and
practice of literature is profoundly influenced by the Baudelairian
and Symbolist esthetics. Perhaps nowhere outside his volumes of
verse themselves is this more evident than in *La Nouvelle origine*. The

statements he made in this essay of 1942 reflect most accurately what is basic in his temperament, in his idiosyncrasy. They remain valid reminders of all that in his psyche was to be permanent, immutable. As he attempts to state his thinking on the poet's language, he echoes the long forgotten ambitions of the Symbolists's "religion," destined to decline just as did that of the Romantics: "Le mot rare et recherché, souvent, ne paraît tel qu'à force de coller, d'adhérer, non seulement à la surface, mais à toutes les cellules de ce qu'il appelle (de ce qu'il nomme, de ce qu'il convoque. Par des mots, le poète (ah! le triste surnom! . . .) recommence le monde" (*La Nouvelle Origine*, p. 37).

Regarding his thinking on the condition of the poet in the society of his time, he proclaims: "Nous reconnaissons que le poète, le ganzo, ce malade de la pureté, se sert des mots dans leurs sens le plus virginal, le plus originel et, en somme, le plus grammatical. [. . .] Ce serait, donc, pour une grande part, en raison de ce puritanisme qu'on accuserait le poète d'obscurité, de raffinement" (*Ibid.*, pp. 42–43).

Concerning his ties with the past, Audiberti believes that the poet's discourse lasts forever, not simply for the historical moment of his presence: "L'activité des origineurs rapsodiques ne vaut pas seulement pour le moment historique où ils écrivent dans un dialecte donné, sous un monarque défini. Je me permets de répéter qu'elle vaut pour tous les temps humains" (*Ibid.*, pp. 44–45). He explicitly states that he will never be heard reproving, denigrating or belying his predecessors. He explains that poets who come to realize that they live so that they can write, operate on a "planetary level," radiating through any "journalistic" and "philosophical" limitations of a given epoch. Interestingly, although his book proposes to be a manifesto about a new origin, he shows no hesitation in rejecting the idea of a "break." Although he never adhered to Surrealism, he could write: "Le surréalisme nous a parfaits. Quelques-uns l'ont intégré. Certains le rejettent. Les premiers, il les a nourris, les autres, il leur permet, plus ou moins, de se définir. Il est de notre clôture et nous l'honorerons" (*Ibid.*, p. 47).

He will go on to assert that poetry and verse must be treated as being vested with metaphysical properties. "Mais un vers, régulier ou non, doit se composer de refus explosifs, véritables claquements de la seconde aux horloges d'un temps qui, lui, ne nous acheminerait pas au trépas physique mais, au contraire, nous porterait vers l'éternité de la vie" (*Ibid.*, pp. 55–56).

Connecting poetry even more with religion, he states in the pages following, "La poésie est l'énergie du monde. Elle est aussi la formule

du sacrement esthétique. .... La poésie est tout à la fois, la petite
soeur, la servante de la religion et l'essence vaste et générale de la
religion" (76). Poetry does not simply participate in the eternal, it is
independent of history. In a startling affirmation he continues: "Des
gens traduisent Horace. Horace, traduit, est en effet actuel. [. . .] En
revanche, Eluard vient de naître en pleine époque Ming, comme
Guillevic en pleine époque Swing" (*Ibid.*, p. 78). Finally, the poet is
perceived as endowed with the powers of God himself, the creator of
the universe. He will not simply "describe," "inventory" the world.
. . . He will write it. Will make it. Will indeed prolong God's creation.

On the question of technique, he prefers to be brief and examine
only "this fundamental pact that seems to be adhered to between
French poetry and the Alexandrine verse." "L'Alexandrin pourra
s'allonger, ou se morceler. Il pourra se calquer sur un thème de
phonétique pure, sur une structure constante de consonnes et de
voyelles.

> Pont d'Albi, sur le Tarn, le coulis, la caroube
> Plantez-lui de ma part le canif dans l'oeuf rouge (*Ibid.*, p. 87)

On the question of rhyme he remains a traditionalist even at the risk
of contradicting himself, as when he asserts: "la rime peut régner sur
l'oreille et sur la prunelle." It seems also a bit anachronistic for a
postSurrealist manifesto on poetry to conclude with simplistic
statements defending the virtues of conservatism: "En somme il est
vain de détruire un appareil, si l'on n'a pas de quoi le remplacer, ou si
l'on n'a pas, tout bonnement, décidé de les détruire tous" (*Ibid.*, pp.
87–88). He is both for those who will practice the regular Alexandrine
and for those who will practice the Alexandrine of dissidence,
provided they are consistent with their dissidence, and for those who
will be guided by the "harmony of their blood," that is poets like
himself, dealing with the "untranslatable." For poets are possessed
with the painful love to dominate, to take everything, to understand
everything.

In his preface written in 1949 for *La Pluie sur les boulevards*, his
ideas have not changed much. Mallarmé and Valéry are still the poets
he holds in respect. To his understanding, hermeticism or obscurity in
poets like Mallarmé are signs of superiority. They are evidence of that
special state of grace Audiberti associated with the poet he calls
Théope, that is the poet closest to God, the poet who uses language
only after having lived it as an experience of supreme mystery: "Un
poète de ce genre, [. . .] n'emploie les vocables qu'après les avoir

contemplés un à un jusqu'à la fascination mentale, dans la plénitude composite de tous leurs sens et sous les références de leur étymologie, et sans oublier qu'ils sont exotiques, forcément, dans leurs rapports aux dialectes inconnus" (*Poésies*, p. 24). The *Théopes* are related to writers only superficially, he explains. They are more comparable to in-layers, floor-tilers, magi or Kabbalists. With their vocabulary, *Théopes* propose "to re-do the work of God," "to start everything anew" and to complete the operation in a state of inebriation, of "genetic creativity."

It is roughly at about the time he wrote this preface that he seriously begins to consider the formulation of his own philosophical credo, under the sign of Abhumanism. In *L'Ouvre-boîte*, he explains in detail how his undertaking to translate Benjamino Joppolo's novel *Les Chevaux de bois* decisively influenced his thinking. Despite its incoherence and its poor inner organization, the text of this *"Colloque Abhumaniste,"* which is a dialogue between Audiberti and Camille Bryen helps us further understand Audiberti's vision and the aims he pursues through the effects of his poetry. Similarly, in books like *Cent jours* and *Dimanche m'attend*, which are autobiographical, as well as in essays dealing with general questions not directly related to the specificity of the poet's medium, Audiberti's scattered reflections point to the same basic fact: With all his awareness of French heritage in poetry and with all his affinities with the Symbolist giants, his brand of poetry is uniquely personal, defying any type of conventional analysis and classification.

Perhaps the greatest paradox in his case is that he is incapable of conceiving poetry outside of fixed forms. For he believes, like Rimbaud, that the poem is the result of chance: "Le poète ne sait jamais comment le poème vint . . . Le hasard de la terre et du sommeil tourne en mugissant sous la housse de poils. Il est sans cesse en train de disposer trois cailloux, un piège de chalumaux, une trappe de rêve. Il captive le poète. Le poète se laisse capturer. Il trace sur son calepin, des mots informes" (*La Nouvelle origine*, p. 49).

As his first three books of verse show, Audiberti went through a period of hermeticism, of obscurity, in which his bias for the phonetic side of language is quite pronounced; he seems preoccupied with intricate patterns of sound, balance and rhythm; he composes poetry as though it were principally meant for the ear; he does not care for clarity; he loses concern for the ordinary processes required for a direct, "economical" transmission of a message through the semantic possibilities of language. He often creates the impression of a dense, rhythmic prose, rather than poetry properly so called, as Michel Giroud so justly points out. Later Audiberti gradually abandons that approach. In *Des Tonnes de semence*, and in *Toujours*, he is clearly in search of a different formula. His metrics display a wider variety of rhythmic patterns, as though in an attempt to amplify his register. With increasing frequency, Audiberti displays the tendency to experiment with new rhythms, often with schemes he never used before. The occurrence of imparisyllabic verse accelerates: "Marble. Siffle. Roule./Mon petit enfant!/Traverse la foule/Attaque. Défend" (*Poésies*, p. 109). So does the occurrence of intricate strophic designs where parisyllabic and imparisyllabic verse of varied lengths are combined (cf. "Gonfle, pointe," "P. L. M.," "Au soldat noyé," *Poésies*, pp. 161, 171, 245). In *Vite guitare* and in *Ange aux entrailles*, the same formal characteristics are combined with a newly acquired, more closely checked concision. Also, nonstrophic poems which become less and less frequent after *Race des hommes*, disappear almost completely from those two collections. *Rempart*, on the other hand, is a "mixed bag," with several pieces still capitalizing on the amplitude of the Alexandrine, the fluidity and rhythmic regularity of the nonstrophic composition, the uninterrupted cadences of the epic movement ("Rempart," "Le citoyen," "Le Meunier d'huile," "La Crèche," *Rempart*, pp. 9, 35, 39, 81). But all in all, in Audiberti's prosodic devices and favored techniques, the traces of his evolution are less striking than the sense of ambivalence which parallels that of his thematics: the almost conscious entrenchment in the polarity already fixed in his first book of verse, between the Empire and the Retreat. In that sense, one can hardly disagree with Michel Giroud who characterized the poet's growth as "l'expansion et la généralisation de son constat critique de 1930."[18]

CHAPTER 3

The Unfinished Tale
and the Tale Without End

I The Novelist and his Critics

AMONG Audiberti's books published to date, there are at least twenty that could be considered as novels, if one adopted a somewhat loose definition of the genre. Such a definition would have to be broad enough to accommodate, on one hand the type of prose fiction fixed by nineteenth century formulae, and which is exploited to the fullest in works like *Le Maître de Milan*, and on the other hand, a variety of unconventional texts whose affinities with historical genres are either marginal or irrelevant, and which are employed under diverse pretexts in works like *La Beauté de l'amour, Le Sabbat ressussité*, or *Opéra du monde.*

La Beauté de l'amour conveys something of the allegorical nature of the *Roman de la Rose* and something of the epic movement of Chrétien's best adventure stories. It tells a simple, sad love story and has the flavor of a folktale. Yet it consists totally of poems adhering to the classical rules of prosody, with meter, rhyme and strophic design all scrupulously observed, enhancing the narration with an unmistakable tone of ritual formality.

Le Sabbat ressussité provides the stage for texts that are "illustrations" of pictorial representations. As such, they result from impulsive transformational processes much like those which, only a few years later, were to attract such "cerebral" writers as Michel Butor. Without the slightest desire to theorize, starting with the famous witches in the beautiful etchings by Leonor Fini, Audiberti's text producing *"atelier"* assemb1ied in this book a sequence of tales of rare charm.

In *Opéra du monde*, the objective stated in a prologue is to demonstrate "the frantic immobility of human destiny." To achieve that end the author proposes to "fix the odor" of the human race, to grasp a sense of the humanity of his time in a "state of anteriority." The massive text that follows is divided into nine "acts," followed in turn by a conclusion titled "Epilogue." In narrative segments of stupendous density, named and unnamed voices seem engaged in endless chatter. In direct language as well as in language thick with metaphors, allegories, parables or proverbs, Audiberti's favorite cast of historical characters is again being discussed in the context of his preferred themes: Moses, Christ, Saint Augustine, Joan of Arc, Napoleon, Judaism and Catholicism, the mythology of pagan cultures and the religions of the East, the world of poverty, misery and crime. In the epilogue, from a department store and a trivial chat between a salesgirl and a customer, the stage abruptly changes to a meeting of a *"Conférence Universelle,"* in a thinly disguised satire of the United Nations. In a fantastic sequence of supernatural phenomena, a destruction of apocalyptic proportions ensues, leaving the department store salesgirl as the only survivor.

Audiberti's novels, little known to the public, are little known to the literary critics and researchers as well. Facing an Audibertian work of narrative fiction is always a challenge. The novelist's message is rarely simple, never comforting. The narrative text is digressive, convoluted, often forbiddingly long. The plot tends to be minimal, when it is not disguised, the action slow, the characters difficult to identify. And yet patient reading is rewarded with discoveries of devices and techniques of unsuspected efficacy and finesse.

As late as 1962, Audiberti does not seem aware of the impact of the major transformations of the genre which occurred in the twentieth century. There is no evidence in his writings or in his numerous interviews to indicate that he read *A la Recherche du temps perdu,* or anything else by Proust. In an interview with Deslandes he observes, "Le roman, aujourd'hui, cherche péniblement sa voie. Elle correspond plus ou moins aux perspectives inédites qui tentent l'humanité: la lutte contre la douleur, la maladie et la mort, les énigmes de la durée, la recherche de nouveaux espaces, de nouveaux points de la conscience universelle, la lassitude devant les drames psychologiques traditionnels."[1] But it is doubtful that he understood the profound implications of the experimentation undertaken by, for instance, the *Nouveau Roman,* in the 1950's and the 1960's. When the subject comes up during his *"entretiens"* with Charbonnier, all he appears prepared to acknowledge is that the new novelists are preoccupied with questions of form and that they are trying to introduce "precise technical concepts" into their works (*Entretiens,* p. 70). His orientation remains that of the nineteenth century, a point he rarely misses an opportunity to stress, slyly hastening to add that he was even born in the last year of that century. And although he can often speak admiringly of Giono, Céline, Mauriac or Malraux and Sartre whose works he can judge with unwanting lucidity, his authorities and the models he emulates are more often Hugo, Zola, Balzac, at least as far as the novel is concerned. One becomes even more keenly aware of the uniqueness of Audiberti's situation when reviewing the critical literature available which deals directly with it. In 1956, the first study on the author's novels, by Henry Amer in *N.R.F.* appeared. In this much admired essay titled "Audiberti romancier de l'incarnation," Amer meticulously defines the essential thematic lines of development in almost all of the novels published as such, as of that date. By its thoroughness and precision, this study remains unsurpassed.

Postulating that, in his prose, Audiberti invites us to a meditation on the human condition, Amer guides us on the meandering paths through this mass of exuberant, intriguingly digressive prose to demonstrate that the disorder and apparent lack of organization in the Audibertian work of fiction is all part of a deliberate, consciously contrived design. He points out that, far from being absent, coherence and unity are, on the contrary, the very laws that ensure, for these proliferating texts, the institutional status of the genre. The difficulty lies only in understanding that Audiberti's *Homo sapiens* is a special breed: "[. . .] l'homme d'Audiberti n'est pas la créature policée, savonnée, évoluant dans les allées géométriques et abstraites du jardin rationnel français si clair, si sage, c'est l'homme dans le monde, l'homme pour la mort de Heidegger et de Sartre, qui emplit ces romans de son histoire."[2] In addition, Henry Amer also focuses on the Audibertian dualism inherent in the conception of a moral universe as well as on the Manichean temptation which he finds lurking in every corner: "La santé n'est qu'un état provisoire une sorte d'engourdissement, d'oubli de son être; vienne la maladie, et l'homme est brutalement rappelé à sa condition, car la maladie est l'état normal de l'homme, la marque visible de son origine."[3] Health, hygiene, good manners are vain as long as the harsh presence of the flesh remains a dominant reality. Which implies also: "L'acte charnel est avant tout consécration du mal, soumission au mal, collaboration avec le mal."[4]

In terms of his treatment of characters, Audiberti could easily be viewed as a Romantic. Amer brilliantly brings this into focus when he points out that Audiberti invariably struggles against verisimilitude to promote "the highest truth." Among the characters he creates, monsters and angels are both present. But these characters are not brothers and sisters of Adolphe. Love, hate, suffering are, in Audiberti's world, always charged with "their weight in blood." Of Audiberti's personal originality, he writes: "[. . .] la grande innovation qu'Audiberti apporte est d'introduire dans ses livres, à la fois théâtre et acteurs, les quatre éléments. La tour de Montaigne, le laboratoire de Gide, la chambre étouffante de Proust sont balayés par celui qui souffle."[5] And he concludes with these reassuring affirmations: "Au manichéisme qui désespère, Audiberti oppose, comme les architectes du XVe siècle, les mains jointes d'une cathédrale. [. . .] Cette cathédrale de mots, c'est la meilleure réponse au dernier voeu de Rimbaud: Posséder la vérité dans une âme et un corps."[6]

It was not until 1964 that a second comprehensive study of Audiberti's novels appeared. It was the one by André Deslandes, presented as a section of an all-encompassing overview. Deslandes' analysis is considerably shorter, less detailed and less rigorous than Amer's. Nevertheless, it covers the entire body of the author's prose fiction, except, of course, *Dimanche m'attend*, which was to appear the following year. What stands out most prominently in this study is an attempt at a generalized, comprehensive review of the thematic content in a fairly representative selection of texts. The inventory is far from complete. As it covers a wider area, Deslandes' study shows already how difficult, if not entirely irrelevant it is to pursue an exhaustive, reasoned account of a system of thought that would stand on evidence of linkage between Audiberti's narrative texts. Through quotations of select passages, this critic points simply to some of the recurring themes: Kabbala and Manicheanism, love, medicine, war, politics, science, religion. In his conclusion, he argues a point that had already been made by others . . . and in reference to Audiberti's theater and verse as well: "Entre la montgolfière de leurs rêves et le boulet de leurs corps, les personnages d'Audiberti se meuvent malaisément dans un univers hostile. La police, les dentistes, les tortionnaires, les Mouchards, les estafettes de la guerre et de la misère investissent le radeau de plus en plus étroit d'où le malheureux naufragé ne peut plus s'en tirer que par l'imagination."[7] Very often they are men of letters or people from the world of theater, like Audiberti himself: "Tous sont, comme lui, dévorés par les hantises d'un monde malade dont les plaies sont à vif: l'égoisme, la brutalité, la haine, le désir."[8] With the remedies envisaged by medicine, science, politics, philosophy or metaphysics proving inadequate, "[. . .] ils finissent par en fourcher le coursier de leur imagination que leur tient l'auteur, tout prêt sellé."[9]

Incomparably better documented and clearly more rigorous is a study by Michel Giroud which also is a section of a book covering Audiberti's work in its entirety. Like Deslandes', this study also is shorter than Amer's. But it has an advantage over both of the others, in that it is comparatively more thoroughly inclusive in its coverage of the author's writings, having been written two years after the latter's death. As for Giroud's assessments, they are basically at little variance with those of Henry Amer, though perhaps a little less categorical. His general characterizations tend to be too vague. Audiberti, the novelist is viewed as unclassifiable: ". . . classique et baroque, transparent et ténébreux épique et réaliste, grotesque et tendre."[10] In reference to the author's novels, Giroud writes: "Son oeuvre reflète le monde, obscur, noeud de questions, concentré de souffrance et de mal mais où souffle une voix tendre qui cherche une issue; . . ."[11] And, echoing Henry Amer, he concludes, "Audiberti dans son oeuvre romanesque suit l'itinéraire dantesque; il faut passer par les enfers pour accéder à l'amour . . ."[12]

The critical approach, as well as all underlying theoretical assumptions in each of the three studies referred to above, reflects the conservative attitudes prevalent in literary criticism in the last century, and to a large measure during the Lansonian era which, soon after the last war came under systematic attack. Amer and Deslandes seem to consider it self-evident that, as an object of study, a novelist's writings would yield their secrets if they could be accounted for in terms of hierarchically ordered networks of "themes." Though somewhat more inclined to deal with the theoretical underpinnings of the genre and related quesions of narrative conventions, Giroud too formulates his judgments as though literary criticism had stood still since Sainte-Beuve. The same can be said of all other critiques reflected in the numerous book reviews which appeared in periodical publications, covering one novel at a time, and which were written by experts: Marcel Arland, Robert Poulet, Renée Saurel, Robert Kanters, Robert Abirached, Drieu La Rochelle, *et al.* Not once has there been an attempt to assess the implications of Audiberti's Gargantuan narrative enterprise either in the perspectives opened through experimentation in the 1950's and 1960's, or in the theoretical perspectives opened through research of more technical nature, involving the applications of a new literary criticism and of a new brand of formalism. And yet, as the Audiberti colloquium at

Cerisy-la-Salle demonstrated in 1976, that is precisely the area in which the Audibertian studies of the future promise to be the richest and the most rewarding. Indeed a movement in that direction may already be gathering impetus by the undertakings of research projects which are carried out in preparation of theses in French universities. Several such theses have been successfully defended and are now at various stages of elaboration prior to publication.

II *Fictions of an Unfinished Diary*

Audiberti never felt the need to publish his confessions in the manner of Rousseau or Stendhal. For all his obsessions with profound ethical and theological questions, he managed to keep his intimate self away from window dressing sensationalism inherent in the genre that appealed to his illustrious predecessors. What he did feel compelled to assert as part of his calling is the function of chronicling events of his real life in the course of an ever transforming, dynamic narrative movement, conferring mythical status and glamour of a literary nature to the most banal, most platitudinous and dull of all texts: The autobiographical anecdote. There is a distinct category of books of Audibertian narrative prose in which the primary aim is to proceed from one realm of fiction to another, to promote the Audiberti myth. Interestingly, in a reference to those of his novels in which the autobiographical element is absent, Audiberti uses the term *"Poèmes,"* and *"élans d'écriture"* (*Entretiens*, p. 124). In a strict sense, there can only be autobiographical novels, in Audiberti's and everybody else's case. But for Audiberti, admirer of Hugo and Zola, Flaubert and Eugène Sue, one can hardly expect the awareness of lines of demarcation normally perceived by a Sollers, or a Barthes, or a Genette even at the time of his broadcasts with Georges Charbonnier.

To the extent then that the author's writings are accountable in terms of conscious, intentional projects, one can clearly distinguish a category of texts in which Audiberti's predominant concern is autobiographical in nature, or of a nature that he would consider *à clé*. Sometimes the narrative is almost entirely without a plot: *Cent jours* and *Dimanche m'attend* are written as diaries. The former chronicles a well marked period of the author's life: July 3 to October 18, 1948, the period during which Audiberti interrupts his life in the capital to spend a hundred days in his native Antibes. The title of the book is explained explicitly as a reference to Napoleon's return from

Elba in 1815. However, there is little in the corresponding events that can be even remotely considered convincing as a reasonable analogy. The latter is also presented as a diary but it offers no definite information on chronology. Neither is it limited to covering any specific period. It includes reminiscences from the author's early childhood as well as scenes from his very recent stay in the clinic, in Issy-les-Moulineaux, during the illness from which, the following year, he was to succumb. There is no plot, no chronological order in the narration. Audiberti reminisces about the main events of his life and about the people who influenced his career as a writer: His meeting with Vitaly, his dealings with Paulhan and the N.R.F., the funeral of Péret, that of Maurice Thorez, that of Cocteau. Reflections on Hugo, Vigny, Baudelaire, Zola, the Goncourt brothers, Giono, Drieu, Sartre. Reflections on religion, on his illness, on the French language and on argot, and on death, that of others and his own.

More or less in the same category are *Urujac, La Nâ, Talent, Monorail.* Unlike *Cent jours* and *Dimanche m'attend*, these books attempt to maintain a distance between author and narrator. In a thin disguise of fiction, the identity of the narrator is not directly linked with Audiberti, but even to the uninitiated reader, the anecdotal fabric of the narrative is a transposition of real episodes and an account of real experiences from the author's life.

Urujac is based on a series of events that took place during Audiberti's trip to the mountainous region of Auvergne. The narration involves a rudiment of a plot and a somewhat more elaborate thematic development in connection with the reality of the man of Urujac, the reality of prehistoric man which is sought in this remote mountain village. In a constant shifting between myth, magic and dream involving a group of researchers on a scientific expedition, Audiberti uses the fictional situation as a pretext for a meditation on a primitive state of the human species, very close to nature, having the purity of its forces.

In *La Nâ*, the narrator is introduced at first as a writer living in Paris. The narration is in the first person and the anecdotal content here also consists of autobiographical notations. One day, a heavy sculpture of a head carved in stone was sent to the narrator's hotel room, left on the floor, without an explanation. The mysterious object soon became an irritant. The permanence of its presence became a constant reminder of all his little anxieties, his fears, his failings and his fatigue. And he could see no hope for relief until he decided to take a trip to the mountains. Predictably, this departure is experienced as an attempt at an escape toward some sort of spiritual liberation and renewal. But the attempt does not succeed. The mantle of snow over the Savoy mountains which he thought could transform and purify the new acquaintances with innocent, simple-mannered peasants and, a ritual of a hunt concluded with the symbolic killing of a lynx, all proved vain. The memory of the stonehead persists, his "inner demons" keep reemerging, even when he reaches Antibes, on a visit to his birthplace. "La pierre Daka m'attendait dans la maison de mon père. Elle était dans ma chambre enfantine. [. . .] Je n'ai pas réussi à manger cette pierre. Son nez s'efface. Ses yeux rapetissent. Mais elle est plus grosse et plus froide que jamais" (*La Nâ*, pp. 358–59). There is very little plot as such. Moreover, the few anecdotal sections of the book are haunted by digressions. The first person narration keeps returning to a meditative mood, intermittently becoming reflective, analyzing the narrator's involvement in the writing process.

In *Talent*, the narrator, Assorbito, chronicles Audiberti's days at the hotel Taranne, in the 1940's. The hotel's permanent customers furnish the models for the author's characters, under fictitious names: Chiniane, the tall, blond fashion designer; Soutrat, the athletic and tender musician from Toulouse; La Valaisane, the bearded architect; the man from Nepal; La Clef, the hotel clerk who is also the manager-proprietor; Henriette, tall, cold, La Clef's daughter; Claure, "the captain," who is a physician, an intellectual with charisma, a philosopher and a guru. The narrator thus can promote the illusion of novelistic fiction by analyzing the people with whom he associates, in this tiny world whose destiny can be affected by as little as the mood of the hotel clerk's daughter. The lodgers of Pompelane (fictitious name for Taranne) are depicted as prey to a special kind of obsession: A kind of "appetite," or "desire," or "hunger." It is a kind of insatiable urge that the word "talent" alone seems to express accurately enough, which accounts also, obviously enough, for the author's choice for the book's title. The word "talent," explains the narrator, is indeed used in that sense in dialectal French spoken in the Cantal region, as it is in the "langue d'oc" area in general. But despite the fact that the author labels this book a novel, it contains no unifying plot.

As for *Monorail*, instead of an anonymous narrator who stays outside of the tale he weaves, acting mostly as a privileged "witness," Audiberti invents a character who becomes the protagonist and thus an object of analysis and observation. Thus the narrative unfolds in the third person, consisting of an emotional self-analysis, while recounting the key events of his life: his childhood and early youth in Antibes, his difficult beginnings in Paris, his first timid encounters with women, his "love life" and his sad wreck of a marriage. In analyzing the protagonist of *Monorail,* Audiberti shows how lucid he can be in analyzing his own weaknesses, his own handicaps: his extreme sensitivity, his timidity, his inability to free himself from the clutches of authority exercised by others. Here again, there is no plot. Only a series of "chronicles" and "digressions." *Monorail,* like *Urujac* and *Talent* and *La Nâ,* is only slightly fictionalized autobiography.

The narrative function is never totally subordinated to the demands of a project that ordinarily converts autobiographical documentation into the mythical entity cloaked in "literary respectability," aiming at that desired status of independence and grace assumed by the work of art. In that respect, the "coded message" of these texts retains a degree of ambiguity not found in *Cent jours* or *Dimanche m'attend.* It is the ambiguity posed by a text in which the narration becomes a self-serving exercise, asserting an absolute autarky of language in an almost narcissistic fascination of the narrative voice with its own fiction.

III   *The Inferno and Beyond*

It is in Audiberti's nonautobiographical novels that we find his best. For if the transformation of the autobiographical anecdote leads to ambiguity as to the purpose of the narrative exercise, or its message, the impulse of free invention and the execution of the process the author termed *"élan d'écriture,"* leave no doubt in the reader's mind as to the author's objectives when the novel undertakes to deal more or less dialectically with a problem of the human condition. From *Abraxas* to *Les Tombeaux ferment mal,* when the shift of emphasis away from the limited perspective of the author's subjective, intimate world of individual consciousness is unambiguously adhered to, the narrative reaches its ultimate amplitude, its exemplary performance. The novels in this instance are of a more "finished" quality. The reader is introduced to representational axes of time and space on a much bigger scale. The decor is enriched through description of travel and changing landscape, often in far away, exotic lands in a foreign country or in mere fantasy land. The anecdote explodes as it strives to go beyond the provinces of the real and the possible, to deal with dream, with the occult or with the supernatural.

Themes and arguments are stated in fiction that the narrative institutes by following two major strategies, more or less consistently. One strategy consists in building a story, with a significant degree of complexity, around a small incident or problem/situation involving either one individual or a couple. The other strategy involves the conception of a grand design, develops into allegorical system, engages collectivities, assumes the proportions and the movement of an epic and results in a text which articulates a message of wider philosophical implications.

Novels composed by the first strategy, which most often have as principal setting the city of Paris, include *Septième, Carnage, Le Maître de Milan, Marie Dubois, Les Jardins et les fleuves, Les Tombeaux ferment mal.*

In *Septième*, the setting is an apartment building in the sixteenth Arrondissement. The novel deals with the pathetic life of Suzanne Oiseau (nicknamed Zoui-Zoui), the tenant of a humble, miniscule room on the seventh floor. Her misery is a lingering, all devouring obsession: she is literally haunted by the desire to possess what she refers to as the "Grand Studio," a large, luxury apartment across the hall from her room. Her attachment becomes increasingly morbid. When given the opportunity to enter the apartment she discovers, to her surprise, that the fulfillment of her dream depends on the ghosts of the people who have lived in it, on the memories of real life going on in it, rather than the apartment itself. Soon she develops an overwhelming attachment for Karoline, the new occupant of the apartment, a glamorous, celebrated actress. And when the latter suddenly disappears, Suzanne is on the verge of suicide. Fortunately, new furniture soon begins to arrive, the prospect of new tenants, thus signaling hope for new dreams and new attachments to . . . the lives of others, the only ones Suzanne is capable of living.

In *Carnage*, the setting at first is the Jura region, the "land of lakes and precious stones" and "spectacle makers." The text of the third person narrative is divided into segments intended as more or less distinct tableaux. In a succession of episodes unfolds the drama of Carnage, a man "full of violence," moved by wild, primitive forces, and of Médie, alert and intelligent, but tender and innocent . . . having grown up like a naiad, by the lake, in almost wild freedom. In her late twenties, she dreams above all of a blissful fulfillment of her femininity. Then the eldest of the Gomais brothers, Carnage, enters slowly into her life. Reminiscent of Giraudoux's *Ondine*, the water nymph who leaves her element to marry a knight, Médie is presented at first as a strangely primitive creature, wild but gentle, symbol of natural purity and vulnerability. But her marriage to Carnage transforms her. In the second half of the novel, the setting is a working class neighborhood, in the eleventh Arrondissement, in Paris, where the couple takes up residence and runs a laundry. Médie gradually turns into a shrewish matron. In his native environment, Carnage was the incarnation of cruel, savage animal forces. He was the killer, the brutal, merciless huntsman. But marriage "civilizes" him, turns him into a moneyed, bourgeois businessman. *Carnage* is one of Audiberti's most impressive accomplishments, owing principally to the rugged beauty of his poetic language.

In *Le Maître de Milan*, the pivotal anecdote involves again a couple and an unfortunate, sad love story. The "Master of Milan" is Genio Stragglioffon, governor of Lombardy, active, intelligent, accomplished, powerful. He is fifty-two, firm-muscled, well-dressed, married—but hardly in love with Bianca, his wife of twenty years— and a "soul of steel," "sovereign," "inflexible." One day he met Franca. Dressed shabbily, she had a wretched appearance and was "neither pretty nor beautiful." She also had an infirmity: she was dumb. But she was eighteen and desirable; the very first moment he saw her, behind the closet door, in a tiny utility room, at the end of an aisle in the governor's palace, he was overcome by the urge to possess her. Conveniently, the young girl showed no fear, and seemed rather eager. There was no contest, no resistance. A consciously shared complicity in an act of otherwise plain, uncomplicated lust—only the encounter was to become the beginning of an affair. Franca lived under the supervision of Mathilde Bracciapelli, her aunt, a filing clerk at the governor's office. Though pathologically sensitive to the dangers consequent to her niece's exposure to male company, she suspects nothing of the sordid affair in which the threat becomes so real with the man involved being her employer. And this is precisely what disturbs Genio. As his uneasiness grows so does his determination to find a way of informing the unsuspecting aunt of the nature of his relationship with the niece. Only the disclosure must be discreet. Mathilde's feelings must be spared. He is resourceful and imaginative enough to avoid unnecessary melodrama. Mathilde will learn his secret simply by reading a novel, *Omerta*, written by him to meet the special needs arisen in the circumstance. Indirectly, in the unfolding of a plot, every detail of his situation was exposed as fiction in the text of this novel. According to plan, it was arranged so that the book fell into Mathilde's hands, which—also according to plan—she then read and understood. To no one's surprise, Genio eventually has had to part with Franca. Life had a lot more in store for him however. His political fortunes already show signs of an upswing: he is about to become the next Minister of the Interior.

In *Marie Dubois*, an incident analogous to Genio's encounter with Franca radically transforms the uneventful life of Police Inspector Loup-Clair. Only this time the woman involved happens to be a . . . corpse. Loup-Clair is a big, husky chap, a bit on the flabby side. He is shy and extremely sentimental. He never cared for women much. In fact, women terrified him. Then came a single unforgettable experience, his first big case. Before he knew it, he was on the scene: a seedy room in Villejuif, where the bodies of two lovers, dead of gas poisoning, lay. In a letter found under the girl's body, a familiar, pathetic story is, in her hand writing, told in moving detail: In the intensity of a passion they both lived as completely, as spiritually and as uncompromisingly as their romantic, arrogant selfishness could withstand, there seemed little else left . . . "Il disait qu'il fallait absolument bâtir quelque chose, quelque chose de merveilleux, l'unité des hommes, contruire des ponts d'or . . ." (*Marie Dubois*, pp. 43–44). So she consented to take the ultimate step with him: ". . . c'est lui qui le désire, et moi je crois en lui, nous allons ouvrir le gaz, . . ." (*Ibid.*, p. 44).

The sight of the "grebe-haired," "white-thighed" young victim was to haunt him long after the scene of the drama. Marie Dubois was eighteen. To Loup-Clair she looked so serene, so sweet, so pretty, that from that moment on his behavior would have all the earmarks of a madding passion. When he launches himself into a long, diligent investigation, it is both on his own account and in his official capacity. But the relentless search soon ceases to be an inspector's inquest. It becomes the mystical quest of a lover. Who was Marie Dubois? A "factory girl"? An "intellectual"? A "high school student"? A "socialite"? All of those and many more plausible images emerge, one after another, during Loup-Clair's spiritual crisis. There simply has to be more than one side to Marie Dubois. When Loup-Clair grows to that knowledge, he has yet one more stage to go through: that of reconciling himself with the fact that Marie Dubois was also a prostitute. The final experience threatens his sanity. But he emerges victorious. He leaves the police force and settles down in a small ruined house where he hopes to live in superior knowledge and wisdom. "Il vit avec Marie Dubois, sa photographie est dans la maison, il a l'air d'aller, de venir, de travailler, de prendre, chaque jour, le train pour Paris . . . ils commandent de loin la terre, les hommes, les grands hommes . . . ils ne sont qu'une seule torsion invisible enroulée dans l'éternité de la puissance et de l'amour" (*Marie Dubois*, pp. 284–85). The interest in this novel lies in vivid, penetrating descriptions of the Parisian flora and fauna, in an environment viewed through Audiberti's memories and personal experiences from the time he was a journalist reporting for *Petit Parisien*. Its main strength remains in the psychological analysis that dissects a man's quasi-pathological obsession for the "ghost" of a little harlot.

Les Jardins et les fleuves, published two years later, also deals with a man's obsession, just as devouring and persistent as Loup-Clair's. The core anecdote around which the novel is built has for its ingredients a set of unusual circumstances that end up haunting the relations between a father and his illegitimate daughter. Jean-Désiré Lazerme, an actor and director/producer of an itinerant theater company , is the protagonist. Armène Béchart was the fruit of a brief involvement with Chatain Béchart, wife of a compulsive swindler, during one of the latter's entanglements with the law. Béchart never suspected his wife's indiscretions but Armène, well before reaching her teens, knows that Jeandé is her natural father. One day while on a tour in Algeria, Jeandé receives a visit from his daughter and before long, circumstances conspire to make it impossible for him to prevent his underaged daughter from following the theater company to Saudi Arabia. In a society of strict rules of moral conduct, Jeandé will soon be forced to consent to a marriage ceremony in the French Consulate, in order to legitimize the girl's cohabitation with him in a country where he had not dared disclose that she was a bastard. This way, the girl, frequently stricken by fits of nervous hypertension, complicated by asthma and hay fever, would have the comfort of his tender care and his constant supervision. And this is how Jeandé arrived at the alarming realization that his destiny had an unmistakable resemblance to that of Molière. By his own assessment, his feelings for his daughter grow in a way that appears less and less simple.

In France he continues to be disturbed, anxiously searching for a way out, when he discovers that his marriage is not legally in order. When at that point he succeeds in persuading Armène to marry one of her suitors (who happened to be a rich Chilean), and leave the country, Jeandé is inexplicably thrown into the despair of a deep, hurting loneliness. In retrospect, memories of intimate moments he spent with her are developing into bewitching, tyrannizing desires.

How will the inferno of this ambivalent passion end? Will it kill him? Will he fulfil his destiny by dying of it, on the stage, like Molière? One evening, immediately following the fall of the curtain to the evening performance, he feels so exhausted he thinks he is dying. Then he hears a knock on the door. Armène is standing in front of him: "Elle avait une fourrure sombre, brillante, soyeuse. Elle avait un bonnet de meunier, noir, [. . .] la tête était belle, ciselée d'intelligence, de volonté, d'ironie. Une femme" (*Les Jardins et les fleuves*, p. 395). He feels triumphant: "[. . .] il s'élançait, vainqueur, dans le primordial jardin où les fleuves coulent avec joie vers leurs sources, lavant chaque amertume, fermant chaque blessure, [. . .]" (*Ibid.*, p. 398). The delicate, tender treatment of incest in this book constitutes a telling statement about the capacity for love of the great performers in the theatrical world, of geniuses like Molière, Chaplin, or Jouvet to whom the novel is dedicated.

Finally, in *Les Tombeaux ferment mal*, Audiberti spins his tale with relish as he resorts once more to a setting of an all time predilection: the area around Nice and Antibes. Although a third person narrator tends to maintain a definite distance between author and his fiction, Audiberti can hardly resist the temptation to deal with a host of cherished, personal memories, dating as far back as his early childhood. Published in 1963, the novel deals with an adventure the circumstances of which become the occasion for another deep psychological study, this time suggesting the possibility of an astounding linkage between love and the reality of death. Lambert Bosely, a famous architect from Nice, has disappeared under unknown circumstances, off the coast of Greece, near Prévéza. At the time he vanished, he was working on a major project for an artificial island while under contract to a large and powerful corporation with headquarters in Nice. His wife Armide, who has in her possession an important part of his papers, decides to hide them in a remote chalet. Unwilling to admit her husband is dead, she stubbornly refuses to cooperate with the corporation by relinquishing the by now much coveted documents. She is subjected to all sorts of pressure, and even intimidation and persistent harassment. But she resists successfully and never does return the dossier.

Her heroic perseverance will be rewarded exactly one year after the episode of her husband's disappearance when she discovers that he is indeed alive. For it is now learned that the corpse that was found in his boat was not in fact his, but that of a young man he had picked up at sea. The novel ends with the closing of a complete circle: Before her eyes, Lambert emerges from the Mediterranean sea at the exact point where, a year ago, he had "plunged" to his so-called death. It is only at this point that the reader realizes that the apparently realistic narration of events was a device contrived to enhance the fundamental ambiguity of the alleged "catastrophe." What actually happened? The question comes up with urgency at the end of the tale. Did Lambert Bosely really disappear? We are now given to understand that the author never intended to provide an answer. We may even suspect that this was all a trick. Is it not possible that, all through the book, we may simply have been in Armide's enchanted Palace, where distinctions between reality and fantasy, the natural and the supernatural, are never meant to be stable or definitive? Audiberti's project of fiction in this book is once more served by the most uninhibited imagination: a project for an artificial island, electromagnetic miracles, strange collusions between policemen and hypnotists, apparitions and disappearances, stunning disappearance acts, all come pouring out of the same familiar bag of tricks that boulevard theater devotees found so entertaining in *L'Effet Glapion.*

IV *The Forces of Cosmic Destiny*

Novels composed by the second Audibertian strategy tend to take hold on a wider geographical setting. Audiberti's ideas on religion and theology find their most eloquent and most rigorous expression in these novels which include *Abraxas, Le Retour du Divin, Le Victorieux, La Poupée, L'Infanticide préconisé.* It is also by this approach to narrative fiction that he makes his most convincing statement as a man of letters: He confirms his fatalistic attachment to poetic language as an end in itself while at the same time displaying his most emphatic anticlassical bias by stressing expansiveness over reduction, movement and continuous permutation over fixity and static design, in any pretext of mediation or representation through language.

The basic trends of Audiberti's narrative style are manifest most prominently in his very first, most truly seminal and by far richest and most ambitious novel, *Abraxas.* As an author's first, it is exemplary in every respect. A third person narrative, it integrates conventional spatio-temporal axes chosen for the effect of didactic abstraction, with a rhythm and tone that promote an overall effect of epic movement. The action is set in Italy, Spain and Portugal, in the fifteenth century. Both space and time are evoked expressly to stress

the transitional character of a certain period in history. The period
lies between the Middle Ages and the modern era, which is about to
be inaugurated into the Renaissance. It is a world which is also about
to "explode" and expand westward by exploration and discovery of
new lands. The central character is Satto Caracasio. At thirty-six, a
recognized portrait painter of prelates, he is burning with a mysterious desire for spiritual uplift and renewal. His best chance at it comes
when he obtains from the archbishop of Ravenna the privilege of
escorting the ashes of Saint Apollon to the village of Hertombreros,
in far away Galicia. The religious symbolism, the allegorical character of the voyage, the tone and texture of the language in the tale
recounting the adventures of the intrepid hero from Ravenna,
amount to an eloquent, almost exhaustive exposé on the lore of
Audibertian themes and devices: the plethora of anecdotal motifs, the
changing of narrative angles of approach, the digressive descriptions,
the long periods, the poetic imagery, and that familiar Audibertian
idiolect here adjusted for the dicta of ceremonial characters in
ritualistic, epigrammatic or incantatory statements of scholars and
clercs, Catholic princes and Jewish wisemen, slick monks and
thieving gypsy tribal chieftains, now ominously grave, now humor-
ous or burlesque.

   In the end of his adventure, at the peak of success, having grown in
wisdom and power, proclaimed Admiral of Portugal, Satto feels
nevertheless an exile, a prisoner. Though he is "cut off from Ravenna,
his mother," the time has come for him to return: "J'aime le Portugal,
ses princes et son peuple, dit Caracas. Mais l'Italie est la nourrice des
hommes. Nourrice ou non des hommes, elle est pour moi la maison. Il
faut savoir à temps rentrer chez soi" (Abraxas, p. 283). The circle will
thus be closed. The voyage will come to an end, with the yearning for
nostos finally undermining the will to move on and to "conquer."
Abraxas may or may not be "one of the most beautiful books of our
times," as Michel Giroud suggested in 1973.[13] It certainly is much less
esoteric than its title suggests. Other than prefiguring the basics in
Audibertian thought and stylistic inventions, it underlines most
effectively the epic character of the author's literary enterprise,
definitely in the area of the novel, if not in everything he wrote, as he
once indicated to Georges Charbonnier. It is no doubt hardly a
mere accident that, in his very first book of narrative prose, his text
begins with this ceremonial opening, echoing the consecrated
formulae for the epic, most revered in our western, postRenaissance
heritage:

Puissances de l'erreur et de la tristesse, puissances de la vérité et de la joie, et vous, puissantes puissances de l'indifférence, ô mère des hommes, ô fille des dieux, consacrez ce livre et aidez-nous. (*Abraxas*, p. 7)

In *Le Retour du Divin*, a narrator skillfully slipping from one post of observation to another, first introduces the reader into picturesque Oustangal, a village in the Pyrenees, where strange, inexplicable happenings are about to unfold. The protagonist is a young woman, Martine, a research scientist living alone in a large house which is also her lab. The story begins with what appears to be, after long years of inexplicable absence, the return of her first lover, the divine Ambroise. But when the couple enters the *"tour gasconne,"* Martine's expertly equipped lab, Ambroise seems to believe that his magician's suitcase contains the instruments of a much superior science. In a stunning scene that follows, he will set out to demonstrate his prestidigitator's skills, creating an atmosphere of bizarre suspense, before he disappears into the night. Lying on the floor, a stunned Martine is trying to convince herself that the whole thing was a hallucination, a product of her imagination, a result of her loneliness. Then in a long series of flashbacks, the story of an engrossing love affair is told in minute detail; gradually linking the circumstances of Martine's first amorous adventure with the sadness and loneliness that poisoned her life following the sudden disappearance of the man she loved so desperately, the fifteen years of waiting and searching, her consuming preoccupation with Ambroise's eventual return. How can one tell what really happened that night in Martine's *"tour gasconne"*? Had Ambroise really returned? Was it all a dream?

In this respect, Audiberti's novel has a striking resemblance to some of Michel Butor's first novels, particularly *Passage de Milan* and *L'Emploi du temps*. For his narrative text, like Butor's, constitutes an exploration of our perception of reality. What is particularly interesting in the conception of fiction in Audiberti's book is the use of an enlarged referential register almost imperceptibly blending in a continuous flow of narrative time, pictorial representation, myth and direct, realistic anecdote. In the symbolism surrounding the theme of the return of the Divine, Ambroise enters Martine's life while he is negotiating the sale of a piece of sculpture purported to be an ancient object of religious piety. The sculpture represents the return of the divine Chamamadai. According to the legend, the Divine was subsequently killed and thus his human form was destroyed. But it was through death precisely that the Divine had just been born. For from then on he came to be known as Ormuzd, god of Persians and Medes. Everything that happens to Martine in connection with Ambroise, suggests an unbroken chain of subtle, symbolic connotations that are asserted and enhanced through the Chamamadai legend. "L'humanité, Martine, attend le divin. Il revient . . . Il ne revient pas. Et c'est leur drame. Et c'est leur jeu" (*Le Retour du Divin*, p. 259).

In *Le Victorieux*, a similar tendency to experiment with the referential registers of narrative fiction leads to an allegorical tale reminiscent of the Voltairian *"conte philosophique."* Here again the approach is ambitious. By acting on the sources of his tale, while narration is in progress, by constantly moving to tap new wells, pumping out fresh anecdotal material, Audiberti abandons most of the ordinary alibis for "represented reality" in literary fiction. Thus the formal arrangements in this text adjust to unconditional subordination, become integral part of a privileged philosophical message: Marcel Colin, the hero of the novel, will be shown to score a final victory in his long struggle to escape from the prison of his dreary existence. He is of very humble origins, being only a modest locksmith from Aveyron. Then he becomes an actor. His entering the world of theater is the turning point in his life, the beginning of a dazzling transformation. First he becomes famous as an actor. His playing Cassacata, the leading role in *Sacré*, catapults him to enviable heights of glamour and glory. The play is based on the life of a living Hindu religious leader, gifted with a prodigious personal magnetism. The public soon starts worshipping Colin as if he were the Holy One, the pundit himself. He is surrounded by adoring women, by mesmerized disciples. But he will be victorious only when the barriers between the reality of the locksmith, the reality of the actor and the reality of the priest are all torn down. For it is then that victory is meaningful: "Toutes les portes sont ouvertes, Dieu est là, et la comédie n'a plus de raison" (*Le Victorieux*, p. 241). The theme of a deliberate project aiming at what Audiberti envisages as the *exit* from the human condition, or from the human reality, links this novel with the dialectic of Abhumanism, the closest Audiberti has come to a systematic, personal philosophy.

La Poupée, the novel that gave birth to a script for a film and to a text for a play, represents another attempt to explore new approaches to narrative fiction. Here too the work of fiction becomes the "locus" for an elaborate formal design combined with a forceful politico-philosophical message. The setting this time is South America, in the

1910's or 1920's. In an unnamed country dominated by a firmly entrenched family of millionaires and military dictators, a revolutionary movement is fermenting. Among the participants are not only the perennial malcontents and the proletariat, but also Guillermo Moren, the all powerful, shrewd and usually apolitical industrialist and financier. Officially, the latter is presumed to support the status quo. The regime aimed at is a virtual military dictatorship controlled by the hated colonel Octavio Prado Roth. Will the revolution succeed? The outcome may well depend on the success of a plot to assassinate the colonel.

But then how can anyone assess the various forces at play in such a complicated situation? How could anyone assess in advance and accurately enough the role of Professor Palmas? This unfathomable scientist appears to be a mixture of an Einstein and a modern version of the Theban soothsayer Tiresias. Did the professor really turn himself into an animated doll, the cabaret dancer who has the physical appearance of Moren's wife? And if so, what role did he play during that banquet in Moren's residential palace that ended with the colonel's assassination, one day ahead of schedule, the day before the staged coup and transfer of power? At Moren's suggestion, it was decided that the assassination would be restaged so as to take place at the prearranged time, at the horse race track, as it had been planned. Coral, the revolutionary who had been designated as the assassin, would now take the place of the victim in the framed attack. But when the young idealist, who, by the way, resembled the colonel as a twin brother, put on the tyrant's uniform everything changed in his attitude as well. Rather than cooperate with the insurgents and offer his life as a sacrifice to the cause, he decides to stay alive instead, to stay in the government palace and be the dictator himself. The "Doll" is elated. The "Doll" was her(him)self determined to kill the tyrant at the banquet. But someone else, an overzealous revolutionary acting on his own, accomplished the deed before she/he had a chance. The "Doll" can now change back, Professor Palmas can be restored to his original, male professorial self. To interpret the message correctly, it is important to keep in mind that the "Doll" was created as a symbol, for "political ends," by a "democratic physicist," as the author explained:

Elle représente deux visages différents de la liberté. Elle possède, avant tout, le pouvoir de dilater l'espace au gré de son caprice et à la mesure de ses mouvements, comme les archanges et théoriquement, les empereurs. D'autre part, pour les prolétaires qu'elle soulève et qu'elle dupe, elle annonce, dans la perspective des révolutions habituelles, la déconfiture des rois, des empereurs, des caciques, des patrons, la fin de la misère et de la servitude. (Scénario de *la Poupée*, Gallimard, 1962, pp. 9–10)

Finally, in *L'Infanticide préconisé*, a complex of subtle issues related to ethics and the philosophy of history are explored under the guise of an adventure story very similar to *Les Tombeaux ferment mal*. The idea Audiberti sets out to illustrate is that responsible, democratic governments can be counted on to act decisively, if by some means the birth of exceptional children, destined to rise to positions of excessive power and become dangerous tyrants, could be detected early. Most likely, steps would be taken to have such children killed. At least this is the message the author is trying to convey, by this preposterous tale, with his preposterous assumptions: what if Edgar Loiflet and his wife Gabrielle had one of those children with the unmistakable *"triplocome"* mark on the right heel? What if the father, when little Felix was four days old, noticed the mark and knew exactly what it meant? Well, if our Edgar were the rich industrialist from Clichy who is also the mayor of Veyssac in the Corrèze, owner of the Loiflet Flour Mills, and his wife were the ravishing Gabrielle, daughter of Catherine Brouillart, the eccentric, cigar smoking widow, living alone with Cacahouy, her excitable parrot, this is how things could have developed in 1935.

And so the story goes. Romain Tapon, a young reporter, is on assignment in the suburbs of Paris where he is studying the picturesque side of "unknown religions." But absorbed as he may be by "Gallican pagans" and the fauna of Bourg-la-Reine, his mission has to be interrupted. He is asked to leave immediately for Limoges to cover a major train accident involving many reported casualties. When he reaches the scene, a series of coincidences end by drawing him into the peculiar drama the Loiflet family is going through. He thus becomes the narrator's witness, an expert one at that, to the extraordinary happenings: Concerned with his son's safety, Edgar decides to take him away from Clichy, to Veyssac, where he hopes to hide him. He knows that the "enemy" sooner or later will strike. He takes the Toulouse bound train and is very worried. From one rationalization to another, he reaches the conclusion that he should abandon the child on the train and return to Paris. When the train derails, the infant is unaccompanied in his compartment. Little Felix is rescued by a young woman traveling with her father, a Hungarian count. And from then on a maddening race begins, with a host of different people chasing after the "pre-destined" child. Among those involved in the pursuit are a mysterious lady in black who succeeds in kidnapping the baby from his Hungarian hosts, two Englishmen tailing Edgar in another direction, Gabrielle and her mother who are unaware of Edgar's last minute change of plans prior to the accident, policemen in France and in England where the last act of the drama takes place. Peculiarly, after a while no one knows who chases what.

And that is precisely when the narrative assumes at its fullest its didactic character. When Felix is kidnapped, a black baby is obtained quickly and takes his place, presumably to avoid complications in case someone noticed the presence of a child in the house of the Hungarian count. When Loiflet learns that the train in which he abandoned his son had derailed, to avoid possible embarrassment he, too, obtains a substitute: he buys a child from a deserted wife who is too poor to put enough food on her children's table. When Gabrielle arrives at the house of the Hungarian count she does find a baby there but concludes that it is not hers. Not because he is black but rather because he does not have his famous mark on the right heel! When two Englishmen pursue Loiflet and finally become involved in an auto accident with him, the baby Loiflet has with him is not Felix but the baby he bought as a substitute. When the chase ends in England, Tapon, disguised as a woman, emerges holding a child; it is again the child bought by Edgar Loiflet in Zoteux from the destitute Antoinette Bouillotte. Who could ever know exactly what happened to the "pre-destined child," the child with the marked heel? Was he possibly strangled and thrown into the Thames?

The narrator who observes the enactment of this drama for our benefit is really equipped to see much more than the actors who play inside the Clichy-Limoges-London triangle in 1935. The time scale of his tale evokes a depth and breadth of mythical order. It has the continuity of the unbroken chain of history. In France, or in Greece or in Palestine—in 1955 or two thousand years earlier—sacred babies were either fought over or killed. And if the children of Jupiter and Venus are destined to become the masters of mankind and are marked on the right heel, then a definite solidarity of destiny should coordinate the itineraries of the girls on rue Blondel, those of Bourg-la-Reine, a Hungarian count and his daughter, an industrialist and his wife, his mother-in-law, Diana, Jupiter and Venus, Jesus of Nazareth, Hitler, Caesar, an Austrian emperor, the Tzar of Russia and Catherine of Aragon and . . . Joan of Arc.

CHAPTER 4

The Savage and the Mystic

I   The Dialectics of Evil

WHEREAS the full message and the importance of formal qualities of Audiberti's verse and narrative prose are still relatively underexposed, his worldwide reputation has been established by the indisputable impact of his theater. Further, it is through his plays that he kept the attention of critics regularly focused on him. It is through his plays that he often stirred lively controversies touching on the more general issues raised by his contemporaries in connection with theater and literature.

To the knowledgeable of the theatrical world, among amateurs and professionals alike, Audiberti's name evokes one of this century's privileged luminaries who conjured the liberating cataclysm unleashed by the poetic theater. His baroque text full of Rimbaldian flights, astounding with verbal discoveries, is made with a material that fulminates or bursts, like a tropical flower. Superabundant, endowed with a decorative, flamboyant and quasi-Surrealist pomp, this text is glittering, vivacious, young, refreshing. Spontaneous chatter, torrential word cascades, phrases that jostle each other and tumble like a whimsical, frantically whirling farandola, everything exudes a strange sort of joviality, a certain folksy, good natured, yet bizarre inebriation. In a rolling of unchained words, in these explosions that blend archaisms with neologisms, erudite jargon—technical or scientific—with dialectal patois—usually vulgar, often unabashedly obscene Parisian argot—by all the exuberance and the farcical truculence, Audiberti, man of the South, effervescent and teasing, molds the surface of a mask on which are borne and alternate a thousand grimaces of an art of derision.

Nonetheless, whatever the pretext for the book he writes, whether comedy or tragedy, what gushes forth at the stroke of his pen and subsequently flows on the stage is the same anxious sensibility, the same profoundly dejected conscience that finds expression in his verse and in his narrative prose as well. His literary vision, his themes and his imagery, all reflect the febrile emotionalism of a man who is fundamentally, irreconcilably, pessimistic. And this pessimism is more consistently pervasive in his theater. It is in the premises of this profound pessimism that the author finds his origins and his inexhaustible source.

There are today some twenty-eight known plays by Audiberti, most of which appeared in the five volumes of theater published at different dates by Gallimard, almost all of them produced on the stage at one time or another. The anecdotal content of these works is extremely complex. The plot is often organized by what appears to be the fancy and momentary impulses of an imagination harnessed by no perceptible effort of willful discipline. For that reason any attempt to summarize content can only lead to frustration, unless one is prepared to tolerate the considerable degree of distortion which is the price for simplification through "reduction."

To the extent, then, that we can take justifiable risks, we can say that the content of Audiberti's theater can be defined in terms of his philosophical premises, in terms of the underpinnings of his pessimism, ultimately crystalized in the sketchy system he called "Abhumanism." From *L'Ampelour* to *La Guillotine*, the spectacle his texts present on the stage is the spectacle of a universe without hope.

As we have noted previously, Audiberti's anxieties and obsessions have their point of departure in a Manichean consciousness of the spellbinding presence of evil in the world. The almost morbid persistence of his preoccupations in this area invariably led him to the outer limits of rational reflection. The problem of evil is as old as thinking itself. It has preoccupied many a poet and many an artist. No less than a real treasure of literary fiction has thus been accumulated, one that might be called essentially "the literature of evil." Following the explorations of this theme in the eighteenth century, the century of Romanticism in France alone has added new jewels to the treasure. The Marquis de Sade, Laclos, Rousseau are followed by Hugo, Nerval, Baudelaire, Kafka, Genet; Existentialists and Absurdists and other preachers of pessimism who analyze the original causes of mankind's miseries follow on their path.

Taking into account the dates of composition of Audiberti's first plays, it appears that the pessimism which pervades them coincides with a vast ambiance of pessimism that reigned at the time over literature and expounded a more and more depressing conception of the human condition. Malraux's *La Condition humaine* had appeared in 1933, Sartre's *La Nausée* in 1938, the same year as Audiberti's first novel, *Abraxas*, where Caracasio made this depressing discovery: "La terre humaine, d'ordinaire, n'est point bonne pour les hommes. Le mal couve partout et partout triomphe" (p. 109). Camus's *Le Mythe de Sisyphe* and *La Peste* had been written between 1940 and 1947. Audiberti's first play, *L'Ampelour*, is dated 1937. The pessimism of plays such as *La Fête noire* (1945), *Quoat-Quoat* (1946), *Le Mal court* (1947), *Les Naturels du Bordelais* (1952) could therefore be considered, at least in part, a manifestation of the general anxiety of those times. But in Audiberti's case, it is not a question of dissecting the old problem, either with the tools of Absurdist dialectics or those of an updated phenomenology.

Neither is it a question of using any other enlightened, contemporary instrument of scientific thinking to contrive rational explanations of the old scourge. Without going beyond the obvious theological Judeo-Christian[1] context, in Audiberti's works, the dimensions of this problem are projected on a cosmic background. For him, it is a question of penetrating a mystery by means of a mystery: It is a question of resorting to the poet's incantatory powers. Demiurge all mighty, the poet alone is capable of exorcising all presence of evil in the world. From that point of view, Audiberti's theater shows that he has learned well the lessons of Artaud's theories on the nature of the theatrical experience.[2] More than ten years earlier, these theories were helping elaborate the formulae for an esthetic of Total Theater which has emphasized every one of the devices and techniques that Audiberti employs in the process of creating his universe. For Audiberti's universe is composed not only of the familiar, tame décor of contemporary life, but also of the enchanted creatures and places of a thousand legends and myths. It is also a universe that contains and integrates the landscapes and collective psyche of distant epochs, of man's remote past. The past is always evoked as a stylized abstraction, but with an overwhelming concern for stark detail in a special brand of naturalism. It is a universe made with a thousand reflections of history: Roman history, the Middle Ages, the Renaissance, eighteenth century, nineteenth century. Doubtless the borrowing of the décor and the adaptation of myths of the past reveal a taste for what one also finds in the best of classical tradition. Yet Audiberti's taste is for adapting heterogeneous elements of his materials in pursuit of a heightened overall effect, in pursuit of shock almost as an end in itself. As we shall see in another analysis (Chapter 7), by cultivating special effects of the anachronistic and of the regressive, he succeeds in adapting his work to modern esthetics.

The first signs of preoccupation with the problem of evil in Audiberti's writings are found in his prose fiction. In *Abraxas*, for example, the reader is at first led astray, baffled by that bursting epic profusion, benumbed with an atmosphere of apocalyptic mysticism. One hardly knows what to make of the bizarre utterances of these prophets in this atmosphere where everything attests, "la grande écorchure et la tragique impuissance de l'univers à passer par d'autres chemins que ceux de l'échec et de la douleur" (p. 231). But in the dazzling, often garish richness of the images of this long text, one after another, the motifs that will later dominate the author's entire work are already sketched. The question of evil is tied with every thematic development. It recurs with so many frequent variations that some critics have likened these works to a huge musical composition where variations of the same theme just follow one another.[3]

Setting himself free from obligations to formal rules of affabula-tion in a rather traditional genre, Audiberti the novelist seems to abandon himself with nonchalance to the torrential deployment of long lyrical passages as if to appease his anguish. He borrows his materials from practically all the literary traditions; he gobbles them up, dissolves them, recasts them. But he remains between the two poles of the same basic tension, often reminiscent of Baudelaire's famous two postulates (one about man's quest for spirituality and God, the other about man's drift toward degradation and Satan). Here and there, his references betray a thought which is a prisoner of its own historical past. Despite the enfranchisement in matters of form, this thought is advancing painfully, often pulling back into beaten paths, hesitating. But a few years after *Abraxas*, when Audiberti returns to this problem in *Carnage* (which he appraised once as his best novel), some sort of itinerary seems to have been completed. The obsession is clearly fixed in a stylistic formula. Having flirted now with the Kaballa, then with Manicheanism, the author reaches a fragile, tenuous sort of coherence, a stage of strange equilibrium.

His quest has run full circle. His mystique evolves into what might be called the poetics of the occult. Médie and Carnage, the two principal characters in the novel, are in many ways archetypal in conception and may be viewed as the prototypes on which are modeled most of the fictional characters he created afterward.

In the symbolic drama played in the deep Jura countryside, Audiberti stages the enactment of the struggle with evil. At the conclusion, evil absorbs everything. The only way the two protagonists can escape is through the transformation suggested by the dream of entering into the nature of the animal world. In the last chapter of the book, Médie finally accedes to the power of flying. She is finally liberated from weight, from matter, from evil. The constantly alternating landscape, the movement from the Jura country to Paris and back, the movement from the laundry shop to the grounds of the *Exposition Universelle* and back, with the passage through the dark tunnel symbolizing the descent to the underworld followed by the flight, everything in this novel seems orchestrated so as to illustrate the essence of the Audibertian thematic dualism.

In this poetry of movement, of ascent, of incarnated abstract concepts, illustrating the incarnation of evil in matter, we recognize a point of departure that happens to be almost identical with that of Victor Hugo. It is a resemblance that has by no means escaped the attention of critics of and commentators on Audiberti's works. Among others, Henry Amer, who likens Audiberti's style to the "scintillating fluidity" and the "perpetual instability" of baroque art, concludes his study on Audiberti's novels by connecting his overall message with the Hugolian theology of *Les Contemplations*. Comparable to his interpretation are those of Jean Rousselot[4] and Pierre Seghers[5] who like many others apply the term "neo-romanticism" to Audiberti's work and insist on his Hugolian side. According to these perspectives, what Audiberti's poetics displays most ostensibly is a vision of the universe where matter in general equals manifestation of evil. Man is the incarnation of a soul which is imprisoned in its "sheath of flesh" and relentlessly aspires to regain the heights of the "great whole" of which, through a process of gradual purification, it is a part. There is little doubt this is a vision inspired just as much by ill-assimilated elements of the Gnostic and the Catharist currents of thought.

Between *Abraxas* and *Carnage* and within the dualistic current which runs through these two novels begins then this dialectic of evil which is at the heart of Audiberti's theater. It is a dialectic that passionately embarks upon the exploration of a problem the elements of which, both material and spiritual, are linked with the origins of the cosmos. For to Audiberti, this is no longer the problem dealt with by traditional humanists, a problem limited to the human adventure. In the manifesto he co-authored with Camille Bryen, one of the topics discussed is, indeed, *"pas d'aventure purement humaine."* In the words of the painter, "une aventure plus grande que celle de l'homme éclate partout. Notre erreur serait de croire que nous en sommes séparés, qu'elle n'est pas interne autant qu'externe, dans notre sang aussi bien qu'en Corée, et dans le Stromboli et dans les pâquerettes" (*L'Ouvre-boîte*, p. 41).

That is in a way the underlying premise in Audiberti's exploration of evil. And the orientation of this exploration is what a comprehensive survey of his theater reveals before anything else. It is an offensive whose thrust branches out into three relatively distinct directions, covering more or less different grounds. In one direction, the object aimed at is the profound disharmony that reigns between what he terms the "Man of Nature," on one hand, and the "Man of Religion," on the other. In another direction, the target is the area of an analogous conflict identified as the disharmony between what we can term the "Man of Eroticism" and the "Man of Love." And in the third direction, the point of focus is the antinomy which itself lies inherent in each of the preceding areas of conflict. The exploration carried in this direction includes the attempt to elaborate the formula of a comprehensive and definitive settlement.

II *Nature vs Religion*

In the first direction, the author's inquiry can be traced perhaps most easily in some of his plays evoking poetic visions of past epochs which also happen to include his most acclaimed theatrical successes, *Le Mal court* and *Le Cavalier seul*. The one play in which the question of evil is explicitly explored for the first time is no doubt *La Fête noire*, characterized by the author as *"comédie en trois actes."* Titled *La Bête noire*, the first version of this play is dated 1945 and, significantly, is introduced by the dedicatory epigraph: "Aux chiens et aux sapins du département de la Lozère." Already in 1945 we see that the author's quest reaches paroxysmal heights in this play. On one hand, the theme of "Man of Religion" is developed through an attack against the "Church of priests," that is, on the formal religion which functions through its mortal mystifiers, the clergy. "Man of Religion" is more than convincingly represented by the grotesque caricature of an archbishop lending his sacerdotal dignity to the consecration of evil. On the other hand, the theme of "Man of Nature" is dramatized by the presence of the young country girls who are disemboweled by a mysterious beast terrorizing the Gévaudan countryside.[6] "Man of Nature" is also represented by an entire crowd of naive, credulous peasants who fall easy victims to a rather grossly staged trickery. Fanaticized against this inexplicable threat, and almost hypnotized, they follow the prearranged movements of a delirious hunt. The ridiculous, ritualistic game which is an interesting replay of the hunt of the lynch scene we find in *La Nâ*, ends with a preposterous massacre of a mere inoffensive goat.[7]

The character pulling the strings at the center of all this is a doctor Félicien who manages to earn the reputation of a hero merely by pretending to be incensed by the scourge. The beast is represented as an inscrutable, terrifying creature, lurking in the bushes and springing out when ready to strike. He attacks unsuspecting, "innocent" young girls, rips them up, and disappears. The man who is given the authority to organize a search, to comb through the woods till the monster is found, is none other than Félicien. Can this neurotic Parisian, this frustrated Don Juan, be the savior of this pagan community of peasants, victimized by a wild animal? Can he be the messiah and redeemer who will restore and preserve innocence? He excites the crowds. He deliberately arouses the religious fervor of the superstitious. When the hunting is about to end, he manages to fool everyone and, at the moment he is expected to kill the beast, he brings the peasants' mobilization to a ludicrous conclusion by having a miserable goat slaughtered instead. Archbishop Morvellon, who happened to stop over at Gévaudan, offers to interrupt his voyage in order to be at the service of the peasants. As expected, under the pretext of exorcising the place, he is there exercising his usual rights over the dupes of the region who are at the point of deifying an imposter.

Audiberti drives his point home forcefully: The idea suggested here is that the "princes" of the Church are not different from the Féliciens of this world. They too are guilty of sacrificing tokens and letting evil run rampant. For this prelate consciously becomes Félicien's accomplice: when he realizes that the pursuit of the beast ends with the sacrifice of a goat he sees fit to let the faithful keep their illusions rather than denounce the imposter and reveal the truth. It is with his blessing that Félicien becomes famous, reaping the fruit of his ignoble imposture. Audiberti seems further to suggest that the "black beast" may be Félicien himself. In one instance he is the one who makes passes at little Mathilde who subsequently, scandalized, wanders off in the forest where she is ripped up by the beast. The beast, then, is evil itself. It is that mysterious, omnipresent, omnipotent force that can be found within each of us. The beast is that force which drove Alice into Félicien's office where they both found their deaths served by Lou Desterrat's arquebus, when the latter caught his niece in the legendary doctor's arms. The beast is the demon who tempts the bishop when he realizes that the hunters are about to kill a goat. The beast is the force agitating the crowd that itself participated in the absurd, ritualistic hunt. And so the beast continues to rip up the little girls. Here and there a weak, powerless voice will dare utter a cry of revolt: Madame Palustre, the candy vendor, witnessing the exhausted animal rounded up by the delirious hunters, burst out: "C'est une cabre! C'est une cabre! Tout par ici empeste le mensonge et le mal" (*Théâtre*, t. II, p. 75).

Alice herself realizes that Félicien is a pitiful vagabond and a rogue. She realizes that in point of fact it is he who is the "black beast." She even takes steps to denounce this man's morbid character. She appears before the bishop and tries to denounce the fraud: "Monseigneur! [. . .] Il faut que vous m'écoutiez. Il faut arrêter cette mare de sang qui coule de nos ventres ouverts. Vous ne pouvez pas laisser le coupable narguer le monde. Allez-vous m'écouter, à la fin!" (*Théâtre*, t. II, p. 12).

Though in the face of this grotesque, irritating deceit Alice rebels, she, above all, remains a woman. And even though Félicien is an imposter and a villain, he is also a Parisian who can offer to a country girl like her all the dainty, sweet, little nothings of precious gallantry. Not that her lucidity is thereby diminished. On the contrary, she is capable of shrewd observations and at one point remarks, "the beast, that's women," alluding to the fatal weakness of feminine vanity. Even Félicien himself, stifled as he is in his painful solitude, can see what evil really is. He is nonetheless crushed by it, at the conclusion of the play, and finds his death by refusing, to the very last moment, to make peace with his passion. In his office, he is alone with Alice who is ready to surrender to him. But the building is surrounded. Besieged by the crowd that threatens to lynch the very man it idolized the day before, Félicien declines the offer of the young woman whose body he has been coveting all along. He tells Alice that he refuses to die in a woman's embrace. By then, confessing that he has always lived in painful solitude, he destroys the myth of his Don Juanic past, and chooses to die alone. This development concludes the play. The episode thus closes on the clear signs of an irreconcilable pessimism and the resigned plunge into the malaise born of the initial conflict. Evil, always there, is an incomprehensible killer, indeed an invincible force.

With Alice and Félicien dead, the insatiable monster ends by devouring everything. The Machiavellian prelate is the only survivor. In the period of Félicien's apotheosis, Morvellon is the real master of the situation. He is the one who really pulls the strings everywhere. Through Bellenature and Desterrat, his spies, he guides and controls from a distance even the slightest of Félicien's movements. Toward the end, Félicien begins to suspect. During a conversation with Bellenature—who, having started as the bishop's valet, is now Félicien's private secretary—remarks with bitterness, "Parfois d'ailleurs, je me demande si ce n'est pas ce Morvaillon de Mordaillon, avec toutes ses étoffes roses, qui tire, de moi les ficelles . . ." (*Théâtre*, t. II, p. 85).

It isn't that the archbishop is here totally identified with evil. But everything in this play that could be considered a direct or indirect representation of "Man of Religion" joins forces with evil against everything representing "Man of Nature." The theme of the inextricable complicity of formalized religion in the race of evil holds an important place in Audiberti's thought and fiction. It appears in most of his principal plays and is always connected with arguments pointing to the duality "Man of Religion" and "Man of Nature." Here is how this duality manifests itself in *Le Mal court*, the play that was the author's first impressive success on the stage. "Man of Religion" is again represented by the clergy of the Catholic Church as in *La Fête noire*. Here also he is present as a prelate. He is depicted with relish as a bishop and prime minister of a Western country. On the other side, "Man of Nature" is represented in terms of the values of an oriental culture, vaguely presumed to symbolize innocence, purity, primitive virtue. The treatment of the theme is also enhanced in a concrete, eloquent manner by the protagonist, the young princess Alarica, daughter of the king of Courtelande.

She is a simple-mannered, naive child, almost as unreal as a creature living in a fairy tale. She is traveling with her governess and her purpose is to cross the border of Saxe and marry the *Roi Parfait* of Occident. In a setting that evokes a literary eighteenth century, she seems to possess the traits of the noble savages envisioned at the time by many a Voltaire and a Bougainville, partly with enlightened lucidity and partly with wishful thinking. At nineteen, cajoled and spoiled in her primitive kingdom, she is already thirsty for the full, sensual life of womanhood. She wants to live "naturally," to be happy with her prince charming. And that is exactly when evil strikes. First, partly out of innocence, partly out of impetuous anticipation, she commits the imprudent act of opening the door to a crafty police agent who introduces himself as *Roi Parfait*. When she has a taste of a kiss the force of evil, unleashed, begins to gallop. When the deceit is uncovered, she is still in love with the imposter who took the King's place in her heart, but at the same time she is torn by a vague feeling of grief. She wants so much to become the most "limpid," the most sincerely correct of all wives. Toward this young man her officers wounded when he tried to flee, she feels tenderness; but at the same time the injustice disaffects her, the deceitfulness of this man who "stole the King" irritates her. When the real King arrives, she only sees her misfortunes compounded. First she is told that the wedding will not, may not, take place. She then discovers that her marriage with the King of Occident was only a political maneuver, a scheme conceived and directed by the Church, the dominant force in Western society. Spain was too hesitant in consenting to a politically propitious marriage between the Infanta and the *Roi Parfait*. The political interests of Occident demanded that the marriage be precipitated and that Spain be forced to make a decision. In a stunning caricature of a diplomat in action, full of zest, the cardinal-prime minister explains to a stupefied princess the staggering reasoning pointing to the political importance of the Infanta's candidacy:

L'Espagne met une égale et constante promptitude à nous proposer la guerre et à nous tendre l'amour. Ses îles africaines, chargées d'artillerie, nous barrent la route d l'or, et, sans or, ma chère, comment se battrait-on? Comment vivrait-on? Or, le roi d'Espagne a une soeur [. . .] Mercédès est encore fille [. . .] Le roi devenant, petit à petit, tout à fait d'âge à se marier, il fut décidé qu'il se jetterait à l'eau, et c'est pourquoi, ma belle, nous eûmes l'honneur de demander votre main à monsieur votre père. La politique comporte plus d'un étage et chaque étage un certain nombre d'appartements. Vous êtes assez grande pour me suivre [. . .] Le Danois nous en voulait beaucoup de notre attitude dans l'affaire des peaux de morue, et Mercédès n'eût jamais rien fait qui put chagriner le bonhomme. Ils se tiennent, dans cette famille, c'est effrayant! Tout compte fait, la peau de morue peut être remplacée, avec avantage, par de la toile gommée. Nous laissons au Danemark les mains libres pour la morue et nous mettons l'Espagne dans nos draps. (*Théâtre*, t. I, p. 158).

She discovers that the young man who has just sneaked into her room is a police agent from Occident. She discovers that even her governess is a spy in the service of the diabolical cardinal. And then an uncontrollable feeling of revolt rises in her. After the shock, she reacts like a tigress. At once she is transformed into a brazen-faced, untamable shrew. For the benefit of the corrupt cardinal who manages the fortunes of kings, she proceeds to do a burlesque dance number followed by a delirious strip-tease. Then she proceeds to agitate the would-be groom himself. As she sees herself caught in a network of treacherous plots, she reacts with a formidable decision.

Evil already flows through her veins. But she understands that evil and good are united by a bond that cannot be broken. She is going to be a powerful, great queen, but, at the same time, a debauched queen as well. She will take full advantage of the lesson she was taught by Occident, the country where the Church reduces religion to a cult of intrigue and corruption. The handsome policeman, the imposter who was the first to give her the taste of a true kiss, will be her lover, her favorite and her minister. She dethrones her father, the old King, whose only assignment will now be to give lessons in the different ways of seasoning salads. It is she who will rule and govern in the future, by means of pride, lust and gluttony.

And that is a conclusion bearing above all the mark of the comic, of the whimsical, of the insanely burlesque. A conclusion which shows nevertheless that evil is all powerful, that it spreads with enormous speed and that no one can arrest its course. It is true that there are no bloody hecatombes of ripped-up little girls in this tale. Unlike Mathilde, Alarica does not let herself be devoured by the beast. She too is ready to show her teeth. She will bite, if necessary. This is the end of innocence, the end of useless purity. She will push evil to the very limit, like the people of Occident, and who knows if she cannot derive some good from it? The Kingdom of Courtelande will consummate this evil in order to gain power and greatness. Alarica is determined to change the face of her swampy little country. She humiliates her father, takes his power away from him, insultingly calls him *"béquillard pestilleux."* The point of this vicious conduct? "Nous aurons nos hôpitaux, des casernements, des instituts. Je m'en moque. Je ne recherche pas la puissance mais il se trouve que je suis la fille d'un souverain et que le renversement de mon âme du côté du mal qui est le bien, du mal qui est le roi, je ne puis l'accomplir, de plus mémorable, de plus exemplaire manière qu'en revendiquant la puissance, par l'assassinat si c'est nécessaire," she intones (*Théâtre*, t. I, p. 197).

By reversing this character's role, Audiberti is hardly proposing a solution. His argument simply becomes circular. The uncouth, primitive princess remains a pathetic caricature even after her conversion to evil. At the point she has reached, the problem must be taken up all over again. For the question again is how far a corrupt, debauched Alarica can go. The antagonism between "Man of Nature" and "Man of Religion" is clearly more direct here than in *La Fête noire*. And here again, the religious element acts as an instrument of the forces of evil.

Audiberti's perception of the duality of "Man of Religion" and "Man of Nature" as well as his acute awareness of the all pervasive, malevolent presence that he calls evil (*le mal*) also finds a forceful expression in *Pucelle*. The author's ideas seem to develop along the same lines, with the same orientation. In this play also, the exploration of the problem exposes the same two tendencies in the same two main components of the human phenomenon. Only in this case the duality is represented by one character only, and the two antagonistic tendencies manifest themselves as two sides of the same personality. Through the fiction we find in this play, the story of Joan of Arc is once again being told, once again distorted to adapt to the formal exigencies of a farce. Joannine and Jeanette, two aspects of the legendary heroine, are represented by two separate beings, incarnated in two different characters by two sisters in a rustic family. The unusual twist is that Joan of Arc, the heroic warrior, the saint, the goddess, France's most revered national symbol, is presented by Audiberti in a somber light. Her innocence, her morality, her saintliness, are being seriously questioned. The youth of Joan of Arc is Joannine's youth. Joannine saunters into the woods seeking adventures with soldiers stationed in the area. She takes walks in the moonlight. She has encounters with Gilbert, the young man who teaches her "Latin," "numbers" and "righteousness." Like an oppressed and sad Cinderella, Jeannette does all the house chores. Of this flagrant injustice is born the scandal, the phenomenon known as Joan of Arc.

But Audiberti extends the allegory considerably further. Jeannette's sacrifice which is the price to be paid for the Joan of Arc legend becomes the sacrifice of the primordial substance of life, the sacrifice of the primitive forces that are the origins of the universe in the beginning of time. Why spurn the flesh which has its rights—just as much as Jeannette has hers—in order to create a Joan of Arc? Taking the argument one step further, Audiberti suggests that Jeannette's sacrifice is not the only price paid for Joan's halo. Joannine is also responsible for Gilbert's suffering. Having fallen in love with her, this unfortunate man is driven almost to insanity while trying to satisfy her outrageous caprices. She tempts him, provokes him, leads him on to all sorts of illusions, all sorts of hopes. Dreaming, elusive, chimerical, she moves gradually away from him. Two victims as a price for a saint is an acceptable bargain, Audiberti seems to reason. It should not diminish Joan's glory. But how can one justify the sacrifice of hundreds of soldiers massacred on the battlefield where she led them? Is she not responsible for all these fighters' blood? After all, they threw themselves into the flames of battle because of her visions. How can one reconcile sainthood with so many dead bodies, with the responsibility for so many victims? Audiberti's answer is clear and incisive: "Sainte de la guerre, on voit mal comment la raccorder, je ne dis pas à l'Evangile, où elle n'a vraiment rien à faire, mais à la doctrine chrétienne. A Jeanne, héros femelle, et déesse du feu, je lui dis: 'Prends garde, il y a du sang à tes souliers!'"[8]

By this poetic "diagrammatization" restating the problem, Audiberti here lends a new intensity to the primordial antagonism between "Man of Nature" and "Man of Religion." The process by which the splitting of Joan's personality is presented as history through creative fiction underlines with implacable lucidity the essential character of this antinomy inherent in the human phenomenon. Man is both Jeannette and Joannine—and simultaneously. On one hand, he exists in the dry, monotonous arithmetic of nature, in the unfathomable mystery cf the flesh. On the other hand, he is exaltation, mystique, religious élan pushing him outside himself, irresistible temptation to deify and be God.

But following this development of contrasts and conflicts between the two principles elaborated in *Pucelle*, the Audibertian quest resumes its disquieting pace and shows again all the colors of cruelty that marked his preoccupations in *La Fête noire* in 1945. The play that best demonstrates his return to that mood is no doubt *Opéra parlé*.[9] As in *La Fête noire*, the action of the dramatic play takes place in the country and in a location haunted by supernatural presences and mysterious forces participating in the human drama. By most of its anecdotal elements, the drama seems to engage forces and characters analogous to those we find in *Carnage*, with the couple Hobereaute-Baron Massacre modeled after the couple Médie-Carnage. We are fully in the ninth century where the advent of Christian civilization has already transformed the landscape: The forests have been penetrated, roads have been opened, cities have been built. Yet the Hobereaute still possesses the mysterious powers of the druids. Being partly a bird and partly a young girl, she lives in the trees and between rocks, but also at the bottom of the lake.

One day her master decides that she should no longer have the magic power that allows her this dual existence. He announces to her that the time has come for her to be married. As with Alarica, in *Le Mal court*, the time of marriage seems to represent a turning point. It also coincides with the triggering of a succession of conflicts. Pure and innocent as she is, the Hobereaute has no idea who the man who was chosen for her is: She is acquainted with the Baron Massacre. Her guess therefore is that he is probably the one who will marry her, since he is the only man who ever courted her. But she is not kept guessing for long. As the events begin to unfold, Lotvy, a young officer, arrives in the area and sets up camp near the lake. The Hobereaute takes him for the man her master chose as her husband. She finds that she likes him much better than the Baron Massacre. When the baron arrives, he discovers that Lotvy is there by authority of the Duke of Burgundy to punish him for the horrible atrocities he has committed against his own relatives and against others in the area. While he is ready to apologize and make all sorts of servile pledges of loyalty and good conduct to gain forgiveness and save his skin, he is wildly intransigent where the Hobereaute is concerned. Whom will she marry? Were the choice up to her she would have no difficulty in deciding. She has already stated—in the baron's presence—that she is in love with the young officer. Alas, her destiny is in the hands of an inscrutable master. Inexplicably, he appears on top of a nearby rock, summons her and puts an end to the dispute—by ordering her to marry the baron.

She becomes a Christian wife, faithful, obedient, respectful of the sacred bond of marriage. She is nevertheless very unhappy. Her husband is constantly suspicious and creates scenes of jealousy. For even though her conduct is correct, her heart belongs to Lotvy. When the latter appears in the chateau, disguised as a monk, she finally confesses to him that she loves him. But she also believes that she has no right to follow him and desert the one who is legally her husband. By her master's law, she belongs to the baron. She had had a church wedding and received the blessing of God's representative. But the woman's instinct in her tells her that her love could still accede to one possible redemption: Lotvy could earn legitimate rights to her person by going to war. She therefore asks him to leave at once: "Va te battre, pour me gagner. [. . .] Va te battre. Mais pas comme un blaireau furtif. Va te battre. Mais pas comme un général. Va te battre je te l'ordonne. Va te battre en chevalerie" (*Théâtre*, t. III, p. 147). She does not yet know that the battle is with *evil* itself and that the only winner is always the dark force of massacre. She does not yet know that in the course of battle it is ruse, malice and hate that win and not justice and love; and that, in war, the Baron Massacre has the advantage.

Indeed the pure, Parsifalian Lotvy, soon made prisoner, finds himself at the mercy of the cruel baron. Tied to a tree, the impossible lover will die of the murderous arrows aimed at him by the baron's *gendarmes*. The tragedy then comes to a last phase when the Hobereaute herself reaches the scene of martyrdom. Rebellious and provocative, she intones to her husband that Lotvy is the only man she ever loved: "Vous n'avez eu que mon écorce. Je suis vierge, vierge de vous. (*s'approchant de Lotvy*.) Je ne fus femme que pour lui. Pourtant je ne sais même pas le goût de sa peau. Je ne connais pas la douceur de son poids" (*Ibid.*, p. 166). In a symbolic scene, on her knees before Lotvy, she will address her final words to him as if his death were a purposeful and preordained act, like the sacrifice of Christ: "Dieu des païens, dieu des Chrétiens, je te tiens . . ." (*Ibid.*, p. 167). She will in her turn die at that very moment, strangled by the baron himself. Evil then once more penetrates the very foundations of the Christian Church, of the Christian dogmas. The Christian marriage, the blessing by the Church, the doctrine involved here by reason of which the ethic of "duty" is imposed against love, everything appears to suggest that the law of religion propagates evil and therefore exists as a function of, and in complicity with it.

Not that the Hobereaute is not awakened in time, not that she did not understand all these contradictions from which she was free while she lived near her lake. She must pay anyway, so the author seems to assert, since she cannot stay in the forest forever. She observes bitterly, "Le Maître a voulu que je me marie, non pas avec celui que j'aime . . . mais avec le Baron Massacre . . . pour que l'Eglise se renie elle-même, en bénissant l'homme et la femme dans le mensonge et le blasphème" (*Ibid.*, p. 150).

And she sees her hopeless condition even more lucidly when the husband to whom the Church asked her to pledge respect and blind obedience becomes a cruel, sadistic monster, inflicting slow, deliberate torture on a dying human victim tied to a tree. The horrifying scene takes place next to the outer walls of a monastery. Lotvy's torture is witnessed by monks and priors who can stand there patiently waiting for the victim to die so that they can add to this atmosphere of calvary the useless hum of their chants and prayers. When the baron reminds his wife of the bonds of marriage sanctified by the Church, she replies, "J'étais une païenne. La plus pure, la plus belle des colonnes de la nature, c'était moi. Mes guides ont voulu que j'épouse le plus affreux, c'est ce qu'ils ont voulu, le plus affreux, le plus ignoble des chrétiens, le plus puant . . . pour que la chrétienneté s'empoisonne elle-même, mangeant son sacrement comme de l'excrément" (*Ibid.*, p. 166).

In the Audibertian scheme of things here, the Baron Massacre and also Lotvy are insignificant toys in the hands of evil and, therefore, its victims. The baron who assumes the role of protector of the Church is possessed by base passions, commits the most atrocious of crimes, finally massacres his own wife. Lotvy burns convents and has the reputation of being an enemy of the Church. He is possessed by a love of which he becomes nevertheless a victim since ultimately it leads him to an untimely, cruel death. As for the parallel with Christ, Lotvy's love does lead to a calvary and to death. Just as the pagan world gave meaning to the advent of a messiah, so the ignoble Baron Massacre and the corrupt clergy become Lotvy's *raison d'être*. But even through martyrdom and death, Lotvy is not able to save the beautiful pagan girl, his beloved. Was Jesus of Nazareth, through his sacrifice, able to save the humanity he loved so much? Audiberti's scepticism on this point is without nuances.

Finally in *Le Cavalier seul* (1955) where he comes back to the question of Christ and the meaning of sacrifice, a process of allegorical composition similar to that found in *Pucelle* gives expression to another variation of the duality between "Man of Nature" and "Man of Religion." Once more the presence of "Man of Religion" is manifest in terms of the Church as a formal institution of organized religion (Christian or Moslem). A Catholic priest, the patriarch of Constantinople and the Ulema of Jerusalem (all incarnated in the same person, but presented in separate roles, in the different episodes of the play) are expressions of the different elements in his character. On the other hand, "Man of Nature" is represented by the Toulousan peasants, stupefied by the mystique of the Crusades.

By its complexities, the adventure of Mirtus, the protagonist, gradually assumes a dual symbolic character. Alternately meeting and separating in his mind are the same two antagonistic tendencies. He is a Toulousan colossus, tall and athletic, brave, intelligent, a subtle debater, he also has a reputation of a great playboy. But, be that as it may, he is a bit scandalized by the bizarre rhetoric coming from his village priest who pronounces oracles and seems to hint at the imminence of miraculous happenings:

> La grandeur couve. Mais les discours retardent l'accord. Moi, je ne suis qu'un petit prêtre. Le baron, toutefois, n'héberge pas que des haridelles pomponnées. L'évêque, l'évêque lui-même me renseigna. La grandeur couve. [. . .] Il faut avoir le tour de main pour déclouer Jérusalem. [. . .] La croisade libératrice s'organise [. . .] Il y a quelqu'un dans un tombeau. Vous partirez avec l'armée occidentale. Les indulgences pleuvront sur vous. Quelqu'un, là-bas, vous attend, sous le soleil levant. Dans deux mois, brave Mirtus! (*Le Cavalier seul,* p. 59)

Mirtus gives in to the temptation to pierce the mystery of this tomb, to penetrate and grasp the truth buried in the Holy Sepulchre. Impatient, intrepid as he is, he saves himself the trouble of joining the other crusaders' armies which are already on their way to wage war on the Saracens, in Palestine. He is thus alone when he launches himself into this adventure taking him first to Constantinople and then to Jerusalem. In the capital of Byzantium, he has everybody in the palm of his hand, including the Autocrat and the Empress Zoé who nearly offers him the entire empire as a gift. Nevertheless, nothing makes him forget his true destination. He simply must see the Holy Sepulchre, whatever the price. In Jerusalem, good fortune continues to favor him. He manages to earn the Caliph's admiration. The Caliph offers him the post of commander of the Saracen army. He also earns the favors of the beautiful Fatima, a very tall lady of the local stock who had nothing to refuse him. Yet nothing satisfies, nothing distracts him. The words of his home priest seem to be constantly on his mind: "Quelqu'un là-bas, vous attend, sous le soleil levant."

Indeed, the moment of testing those utterances is not very far. A man wearing a crown of thorns and pronouncing strange words appears before him. Soon afterward, the same man is arrested by the police and treated as a criminal. That is when the intriguing suggestiveness of these circumstances becomes a source of anguish for Mirtus and a serious challenge: Who can that man be? Is he really a criminal? Is he Jesus Christ? Hardly has he time to think when he is informed that the mysterious captive is about to be impaled. During a game of chess that he plays with his friend the Caliph, he witnesses this man's tortures in an allegorical reenactment of the Holy Passion. And it is at this point that Mirtus's illusions begin to crumble. When he sees the prisoner pass by, when he hears him cry, "J'ai soif . . . J'ai soif . . . Je voudrais être hors de la souffrance," he bursts out:

> Brusquement je comprends. Rien n'avait eu lieu [. . .] C'est dans cet endroit, c'est en ce moment que la Passion s'accomplit [. . .] Comprenez-moi. Je doutais de mon église parce que je l'avais vue, elle, avant de le voir, lui . . . Maintenant, je sais que c'est véritable . . . D'un seul coup, tout me remonte . . . La Pentacôte . . . La Chandeleur . . . La fête des Rameaux. . . . Tout est en train de se passer . . . Pas tout à fait comme on nous l'a conté, mais peut s'en manque [. . .] Tout ce que Dieu veut, c'est un verre d'eau. Dieu le veut! C'est rentrer chez lui qu'il veut. C'est se coucher. C'est qu'on le délivre du mal. (*Ibid.*, p. 226)

And what is worse is that he, the Christian knight, will be unable to deliver his God from evil. First he asks the Caliph to pardon the prisoner. Then he proposes that the prisoner be the ante of their chess game. Ironically, when told that all he has to do to save the condemned is to die in his place, he finds himself unprepared for the sacrifice.

But he does feel all the pain that a coward's conscience can inflict. His voice is tense with despair: "Venez me délivrer. Je suis l'homme. Je suis Mirtus. Je suis mon propre tourment. . ." (*Ibid.*, p. 236). Why had he thought that he had come to Palestine only to discover that the tomb did not exist? "J'étais venu . . . J'étais un chevalier trousseur. Je ne croyais pas dans le père. Je ne croyais pas dans le fils. J'avais giflé ma mère. J'avais raison. Dans la maison du maître éternel, il n'y avait personne. Maintenant, il y a quelqu'un" (*Ibid.*, p. 235).

He now knows that this someone is none other than his own self. His adventure was now coming to an end, his quest, completed.

The epic grandeur of Mirtus's undertaking dramatizes the duality between "Man of Nature" and "Man of Religion" perhaps in its most abstract form of universality. Viewed in its concrete forms through its Christian references, the problem of evil is shown here as an absurd, insurmountable wall against which the two faces of humanity are perpetually dashed. And at the conclusion of the Audibertian analysis, evil as a principle of primordial order asserts itself as the only deity capable of an effective presence in the universe.

Over the spellbound world evoked by the works just surveyed, the shadow of a demonic presence is cast, the specter of a malefic power emerges and makes itself felt. The locus where its energy acts and proliferates is the universe of man, that vulnerable affectivity, that pluralistic, alert sensitivity which is unable to immunize itself against suffering. Being essentially flesh, "Man of Nature" is never successful in his attempts to escape physical pain. Being above all an ambitious aspiration to restore a contact with his source and first origin, to merge with the all powerfulness of the divine, the one and only secret to Edenic beatitude, "Man of Religion" fails to discover the mantic formula that might restore a longed for unity with everything that lies beyond the flesh. By yielding perpetually to the temptation of the divine, he becomes the author of his own suffering, the very mechanism of his own destruction, and therefore the instrument of evil. Thus in the Mathildes and the Morvellons, in the Alaricas and the wheeling and dealing cardinals, in the Mirtuses and the sorcerer-priests of the Crusades, in all these engaging expressions of the human drama, the omnipresence of evil is affirmed. "Man of Nature" and "Man of Religion" consummate their antagonism in an ocean of suffering, asserting here the old, almost forgotten, premises of preAugustinian, Manichean theology.

CHAPTER 5

Eroticism Versus Love

I *Interdiction and Transgression*

THE second direction in which Audiberti's exploration is advanced is equally visible in most of his plays. His main point of focus being the discord between the "Man of Eros" and the "Man of Love" in the situations orchestrated by the poet in his theater, eroticism and love are often the only principles available to command the deployment of characters and dramatic action. On the other hand, almost equally often, they are complementary or subordinated to their homologous principles of nature and religion discussed in the preceding chapter. But however varied the circumstances, these principles are always in conflict. In fact they exist by virtue of that very conflict. By a baffling whim inherent in the great paradox that human nature seems to be, a fatal necessity of perceiving and judging in time and in space unfailingly conditions their coexistence and their incompatibility in such a way that their coming into being automatically triggers their rigorous antagonism.

As with nature and religion, this fatalism is invariably represented by the sinister shadow of evil. It is consistently evoked at every stage of the mythopoeic process in nearly every play. The references are in most cases unequivocal. In fiction, "Man of Eros" and "Man of Love" are evidenced as two forces incarnated quite frequently in the same individual character. But most often they are demonstrated as two tendencies existing separately in the individual members of a heterosexual couple. Their role thus becomes very concrete in connection with the reality of the human couple, in the sexual interaction between male and female. The human phenomenon is in this case envisaged on the same differing planes of reality as it exists on for the sexual being who, torn apart from the fundamental unity, struggles for survival "dialectically," so to speak, by an effort toward integration pursued on a cosmic scale.

Needless to say, in Audiberti's time, love and eroticism in "consecrated" literature are commonplace even by postSurrealist criteria. In itself, the presence of these themes in the works of a Southern poet, so proud of his Provençal and Felibrian heritage, could not mean anything out of the ordinary. What is noteworthy or, to put it more accurately, phenomenal, is the manner in which these themes are presented and developed in a profusion of poetry which integrates them in patterns illustrating a personal philosophy. As they emerge from the phantasmagoria of a seemingly inflated and frivolous décor, under a camouflage of dizzying juxtapositions of the cruel and of the drole, the macabre and the preposterous, the terrifying and the ludicrous, these themes bear witness of an unequal lucidity, filtered through an all too unique force of temperament. Before quite reaching the reader's attention, these themes are concealed, disguised, twisted and untwisted a thousand times, as in a maddening, whirling dance. Arrested in the movement of its continuous metamorphosis, this style represents each time some sort of alchemy whose formulae, now elusive, now brazenly assertive, seem to embrace all the secrets of the cosmos.

There would be no difficulty at all in tracing the literary origins of such trivial themes as "eros" and "love" in the dramatist's works. Distant echoes of a precious heritage, they are discernible in delectable evocations of medieval folklore. Likewise, they can be identified in terms of their obvious links with the myths of the Romantics with whom the author has a substantial affinity both in temperament and philosophical orientation. Again and again, we recognize the direct references to the same elements of the same source of anxiety that perturbed Musset and Baudelaire, Michelet and Lautréamont. With an equal avidity, Audiberti the poet draws on a well-familiar rhetoric of love. It is the rhetoric typical of the ideologically colored, bold Romantic literature of the first half of the nineteenth century as well as that of the second half, and that of the so-called "decadent" literature. Finally, on the whole, the influence of the Surrealist thematics, particularly that of Benjamin Péret, perhaps more than any other, is clearly noticeable. Making allowances for a somewhat sketchy summarization, we can distinguish in Audiberti's works what can be described as a dialectic of eroticism and love, the pace and direction of which are entirely subordinated to the hold of evil, and in total accord with the well-known Surrealist point of departure: "Le 'mal' pour Lautréamont (comme pour Hegel) étant la forme sous laquelle se présente la force motrice du développement historique, il importe de le fortifier dans sa raison d'être, ce qu'on ne peut mieux faire qu'en le fondant sur les désirs prohibés, inhérents à l'activité sexuelle primitive tels que les manifeste en particulier le sadisme."[1]

The line of this anguished dialectic runs through almost every one of the author's books, from his first collections of poems to his last novels, from *L'Empire et la Trappe* to *Dimanche m'attend*. It appears frequently also in his essays, carried on through sometimes chapter-long arguments in a discursive and explicit manner. Marvelling at the mysteries of procreation, at the female physiology, anatomy and idiosyncrasy, the poet is repeatedly drawn into self-indulging dissertations on the mechanics of sexuality. Here is an example taken at random from *L'Abhumanisme:*

> On voudrait ne pas blasphémer. Mais comment ne pas voir, dans l'idéalisme de l'amour, l'effet d'un édit général aux termes duquel nos comportements organiques se couronnent, toujours, d'une transparente volute qui, sous couleur de les confirmer, les désavoue?... C'est sur l'appareil extérieur de l'amant que se précipitent et s'accumulent nos pensées effarées relatives à la végétale bestialité de l'outillage érotique naturel. Mais, dans leur justice ces pensées ne tardent pas à délaisser ce mât de cocagne naïf pour se poser non sur l'endroit gynécologique correspondant, mais à même le corps tout entier de la femme. (pp. 118–19)

Fairy tale creatures, disintegrated, irreducible to any manner of psychological coherence, the characters of his theater are tormented by the fixations and traumas resulting from unresolved antagonisms between the two tendencies. On one hand, eroticism by itself is an impenetrable enigma to begin with. Its *raison d'être* is a biological inevitability which keeps it constantly under the yoke of pure sexuality, on the animal level. But, the human animal is also a social being. Audiberti never tires in reminding us how, in the social framework, restrictive forces multiply quickly in the form of direct or indirect prohibitions. A sort of erotic protocol is so created. How are the norms of eroticism born? What is the nature of the necessity that dictates them? Those are some of the questions that haunt the author. And in his anguished quest invariably we find only one answer which marks the *dénouements* of practically all of his plays dealing with the subject. It is that both eros and love, impulses of an inner being, are initiated and controlled by only one supreme, omnipotent deity: Evil.

To examine the concrete modes of manifestation of this exploration in the author's dramas, we need only analyze two relatively distinct areas: In the first one, we can approach this question merely as a moral crisis brought on as a result of a tension within the ethical conscience by and large between an "interdict" and a "transgression." In the second, we can deal with a more complex aspect of the issue, namely the question of the Don Juan complex and, in addition, the rapport that eroticism and love have, in Audiberti's theater, with many types of aggression, including the homicidal impulse.

Concerning the first area then, and the problem of the moral sensitivity, what we observe principally is that Audiberti is seriously preoccupied with the different forms this sorcery establishes in the conscience of the sexual being such as taboos, or "interdictions." His malaise is shown poignantly in several plays where the dramatization of this extremely complex problem is often marked with hallucinatory intensity. To begin, let us first take the case of *Quoat-Quoat*.

The presence of evil is unmistakable. By the usual means of witchcraft-like atmosphere, the ubiquitous, malefic force is active here through the Aztec god Quoat-Quoat.[2] As is the case in several other plays, this configuration of evil here also emerges from a pagan legend, from the distant, primitive past. Thus the empire of this deity is here suddenly extended over the destiny of the steamship Mirmidon, which has just set sail for Mexico. The allegorical nature of the voyage is carefully underlined: The Mirmidon represents the universe, both as a poetic image and as a theological concept. It is a vessel that can be powered by a steam engine—but also uses its sails. Its strength then comes both from within and from an outside source. Amédée, the protagonist, is one of the passengers, a young man, travelling as a government agent. Aboard the Mirmidon, he introduces himself as an archeologist, but his true mission is to go to Mexico and search for Emperor Maximilian's treasure. It is only a few moments after he has boarded the ship, that the terror of Quoat-Quoat's bewitching energy begins to come unleashed and take over. In a sustained nightmarish atmosphere, the captain of the ship calls on Amédée in his cabin and explains the ship's regulations: If a secret agent brings a woman on board, the captain is required first to have his fingernails pulled and then to have him shot. If the said agent starts an affair with a woman during the voyage, the consequences will be the same. The regulation is not absurd, at least according to the captain, who explains: "l'intimité du couple ronge le noyau de l'homme." At first comical or clownish, the captain's weird interpretations of the ship's regulations become more and more disquieting, aimed at frightening the young man into a state of panic. But he insists the regulations are for Amédée's protection, in view of the seriousness of his mission. "Prenez une maîtresse. Vous l'appellerez mon trésor. Le trésor alors, adieu! Plus vous y réfléchirez, plus il vous apparaîtra comme à moi, que le réglement semble fait pour vous. Il vous gante des pieds à la tête. Vous pouvez dire qu'il vous va!" (*Théâtre* I, p. 18).

Will Amédée escape from this trap? What power does he have over circumstances determined either from the outside or from the pressures of an overflowing euphoria caused by the biological functions of his youthful existence? "J'ai vingt-six ans. Que diable. J'ai des yeux. J'ai des mains. Dependant, d'après vous, si j'embrasse, je meurs! Les femmes, par vos soins deviennent des chiennes enragées, des vipères" (*Ibid.*, p. 20).

It so happens that some rather appetizing samples of the female sex are available on board: Beautiful French girls, attractive South American girls, intoxicating creoles! Amédée is by coincidence the only young bachelor on board. Will he be able to insist on casual, superficial relationships? On that score, the captain hastens to explain that between different kinds of relationships, as far as he is concerned, the lines of demarcation are clear: "On est coupable ou on ne l'est pas. Quand on l'est, ça se sent, ça se voit, et l'intéressé lui-même ne s'y trompe pas. Vous ne vous y tromperez pas. Le bien et le mal, le sentiment du bien et du mal, c'est là-dedans que ça se fabrique. (Il montre le ventre d'Amédée)" (*Ibid.*). And he goes on to specify that his experience as captain makes him "capable de distinguer entre un baiser qui n'engage que des sympathies charnelles, bestiales, . . . et des échanges et des contacts qui, même plus subtiles, plus anodins, un coup d'oeil, un frémissement, révéleraient une complicité profonde, pernicieuse" (*Ibid.*).

The distinction made in those terms by the captain between pure sexuality and eroticism makes Amédée's situation even more problematic. For as chance (which is here identified by Quoat-Quoat's demonic will) is about to determine, Amédée meets the captain's daughter in whom he recognizes Clarisse, his childhood sweetheart. It is then only a matter of time before the captain witnesses a blatant infraction and rushes to enforce the sinister regulation: Amédée will be shot the following day at four o'clock in the morning. With the encounter of these two youths, a dream of love begins to grow. Such as Amédée conceives it, this love puts him "out of reach of even the shadow of the Catholic God's hand." In his moment of ecstasy, he will be carried far away from the reality of either sexuality or eroticism. But the same moment will nurture the dream of his city made of light, to be erected from the very ruins of Quoat-Quoat's temple. Turning to Clarisse, he intones,

> La tête du dieu Quoat-Quoat est là. Elle est rouge . . . De part et d'autre de la tête se dressent les colonnes royales. Tant de soleils ont passé sur elle que les lèvres se sont usées, que les prunelles se sont vidées . . . goûter dans ce lieu de la plus majestueuse détresse un amour comme le nôtre, tout excité d'un souvenir de campagnes fraîches en Normandie, d'églises rustiques du côté d'Orléans, c'est plus fort, c'est plus âcre, Clarisse, toi mon amour! que tous les péchés réunis. (*Ibid.*, pp. 33-34)

Nonetheless, the all-powerfulness of evil symbolically represented here by Quoat-Quoat remains unchallenged. Amédée probably can somehow stay out of reach of the arm of the savage God. By his revolt against the absurd dominion of Mirmidon's regulations, in a way he can place himself beyond the captain's power. For, at the moment his execution order. Alas, it is a futile revolt.[3] The forces that were set in motion for this adventure to take place and to end so pathetically that it is she who is the secret agent, not Amédée. The latter is simply a straw man, chosen without his knowledge for diversion. All of a sudden he becomes aware of the extent to which he is at the mercy of circumstances he does not control. Not unlike Camus's absurd hero, Amédée refuses to capitulate to the whim of chance. As he is pardoned, when his identity is revealed, he braves again the captain's decree and offers himself voluntarily to the bullets of the gendarmes who, unaware of the last development, were waiting to carry out the execution order. Alas, it is a futile revolt.[3] The forces that set in motion for this adventure to take place and which end so pathetically originate in a source that is outside of the Mirmidon and beyond her captain's authority. The prisoner's gesture transcends the jurisdictional questions related to the ship's code or to the regulations governing her passengers' conduct. Obviously it also makes a mockery of the captain's authority which was, as of that day, believed to be boundless. When the captain realizes the full implications of that unexpected self-immolation, his disillusionment comes to him as a crushing shock. In the terror of his awakening he will throw on the floor of his cabin Quoat-Quoat's sacred stone, a fetish that keeps in chains the Aztec god's occult powers, and the Mirmidon will be blown to pieces.

Eroticism and love viewed as two tendencies incurring head-on collisions with "interdicts" are the mainsprings of more than a few of

Audiberti's characters. Aside from the characters in *Quoat-Quoat*, we could cite those in *Le Mal court*, those in *Opéra parlé* and *La Fourmi dans le corps*. In *Le Mal court* that we examined from a different viewpoint in the preceding chapter, Alarica's conversion results from an awakening to eroticism. Part of the Cardinal's Machiavellian scheme consists in luring the princess into a trap where she is kissed by a young man posing as the *Roi Parfait*. It is with that kiss that the mechanism causing evil to start on its rampant gallop is triggered. For it represents the transgression that the Occidental culture considers unpardonable, and which arouses the nagging consciousness of insipid, indeterminate, guilt. The princess' love dream is soiled. And yet it is in this imposter who appears in the early dawn that the princess recognizes the true face of love. He enters like a storm, he kisses her, he tells her "my whole being flows out of you." How could the transgression be anything but an inexorable necessity? When the true King arrives, she finds he is not a knight in shining armor. He is instead, a little silly, a little pedantic, a little fat and submissive to his prime minister, as a little boy is to his schoolmaster. Ostensibly, the innocent princess is awakened to a reality that shatters her every dream, putting an end to any kind of hope for the idyllic, princely love she thought so near. The hand that guides the events of such a world can only be that belonging to evil, that same malefic deity who in *Quoat-Quoat* appears as a specter of the Aztec god.

It is this very same power that also controls the Hobereaute's destiny in *Opéra parlé*. Only there the god Quoat-Quoat is named *Maître Parfait*. It is by his inauspicious game that the Hobereaute is awakened to the so painful consciousness of womanhood. Just as Alarica's dream dissipates between the *Roi Parfait* and his impostor, so does the Hobereaute's between Lotvy and the Baron Massacre. The guilt in the Hobereaute's transgression is just as inevitable as that in Alarica's. One day it is announced to her that the moment has come for her marriage. That is an announcement made to all young girls sooner or later by the same mysterious voice of nature which from that point on, Audiberti suggests, starts to nourish the dream of the impossible love. The Hobereaute recognizes her face when she encounters the handsome Lieutenant Lotvy. The Baron Massacre, destined for her by her master, is a monstrosity of physical and moral ugliness. And yet she had been forced to renounce her dream and make of ugliness a life-long companion.

Elsewhere, in a strictly Platonic treatment of the subject, an equally absurd fatality frustrates the dream of love possessing the sublime

Eleonora, torn between the warrior Salvatico and the poet Torquato Tasso: In *Altanima*, the most atypical[4] of Audiberti's plays, the fulfillment of a prophecy in the warrior's death chains her destiny with a burden of tragic guilt when she releases Salvatico from an oath to abstain from war!

Finally, the same oppressive fatality is the inescapable lot of Barthélémy de Pic-Saint-Pop, the heroine in *La Fourmi dans le corps*. Here, too, the problem of interdiction and transgression is explored in connection with the conflictual aspects of eroticism and love. The protagonist is a seventeenth century lass. She is intelligent, sophisticated, arrogant and . . . a virgin. She belongs to that frolicking, reputedly fun loving society of the century, known to be "libertine," but not debauched. As the author explains it, the *"libertins"* "Ce sont des intellectuels en quête d'un sens rigoureux à donner à la vie." They are fond of "les maîtres qui nous enseignent l'ironie et les philosophies qui méprisèrent l'amour" (*Théâtre*, t. IV, p. 136).

But this presumably blasé woman begins her adventure by slighting and deliberately refusing eroticism under the pretext of higher philosophical preoccupations. It is a familiar posture. Barthélémy decides to withdraw from the world, to retire into Remiremont, "a politically sovereign state, administered by a chapter of nuns," as the author explains in an introductory *"résumé"* (*Ibid.*, p. 129). This community is in itself an autonomous independent world, a universe cut off from all the rest. At least that's what Barthélémy believes. There she hopes to find her fulfillment by leading a life that can be free of the temptations of the flesh. As she states to the canoness' coadjutrix who welcomes her, the reason for her retreat is "le désir d'échapper au désir" (*Ibid.*, p. 147).

But in this sheltered world that she believes insulated from the animalistic baseness of sexuality, she discovers that one half of the canonical population consists of worldly ladies, "pas davantage astreintes au célibat que n'importe quelle femelle non clôturée et qui n'ont peur des prêtres ni des chevaux" (*Ibid.*, p. 144). She will even happen to sit in at a secular, pagan and Dionysian feast which was organized by the "bees," the scandalous nuns. It is true that her trooper's temperament will prevail, that she will fight and even take command of the struggle on the side of the "ants" who are the nuns opposing the "bees." But at the crucial moment a new element is introduced into the battlefield. It turns out that Remiremont is not quite as unaffected by the outside world as it first seemed. Despite its apparent political independence, this universe too has its Quoat-Quoat. His presence is here manifest in the palpable reality of none other than the great Turenne. The war rages all around Remiremont. The illustrious marshall who has just defeated the German troops in Alsace decided to camp in this town. The action unfolding becomes now again a sketchy allegorical game.

Provoked by two "ants" who fire a cannon shell at his tent, Turenne threatens to tear down and burn everything standing in Remiremont. And all would be lost if Barthélémy did not discover, by accident, the presence of what she thought an abandoned tiny baby in her room. In front of this miniscule male, the Platonist philosopher is taught a lesson about life, about the rights of the flesh, about tolerance and hope. In Audiberti's rhetoric on this subject, this means that she submits to the rule of evil. She discovers that her friend du Marquet, whom she considered a *"libertin"* nurtured with Seneca and Plato, wears an officer's uniform and makes war for the King of France. And in wartime evil runs fast . . . among intellectuals and among virgins. Her reaction is extreme and matches that of Alarica in the conclusion of *Le Mal court*. She demands to be raped at once by this vagabond, and, of all places, in Turenne's bed! When the little dosser containing the infant that triggered her conversion was brought to her, she discovered with horror that the little boy had been replaced by a grotesque looking dwarf. Her spiritual transformation was now complete. She will reconcile herself with the necessity of a new existence. She will show this with her last gestures, with the acceptance of the little monster as her adopted son, and of Du Marquet as her husband. The marriage that concludes Barthélémy's adventure, just as Alarica's alliance with the imposter who seduced her, eloquently highlights Audiberti's treatment of this subject with poignant irony.

II   *On the Don Juan Complex*

With regard to the second area of our analysis, the terrain is much darker, much more depressing. Audiberti's exploration assumes an almost delirious pace and often leads to the remotest, the most intimate recesses of the human psyche. The point of departure here no longer is a conflict in the conscience of "interdictions" and "transgressions." Eroticism and love, in this case, destroy the fundamental, the functional unity of the ego, either by reason of prolonged, unresolved conflict or by reason of total alienation. In the language of poetry and fiction of this theater, the frenzied anomalies often have such an effect on the subject's personality that the equilibrium of all mental functions is broken. What follows then is the pathological extreme of an obsession which evolves as an uncontrollable expansion. The behavior in which this expansion becomes perceptible appears in variations of what might be called the "Don Juan complex," or in specific patterns of criminality.

Let us begin with the case of Félicien, the protagonist of *La Fête noire*. He is timid and withdrawn. The reason he leaves the big city (Paris) is that he wants a chance to understand his ineptitudes, to find some answer both to his inferiority complex and to a haunting suspicion of impotence. He approaches innocent, naïve, peasant girls who might be attracted by what he seems to advertise as the refinement of the mundane Parisian. He actually never had any success with women. He lacks something basic, but does not quite know what it is. Will he find it some day? He is determined to keep looking. Only while his search goes on, his anguish increases. We have already seen to some extent his role in the famous hunt of Gévaudan. He had succeeded for quite a while in mystifying the peasants into believing that he was sent by divine Providence and that he was their salvation. What is the nature of the source of energy behind all that activity? To put his message across, Audiberti evokes with this character a whole complex of specific malfunctions, translating his own intuitions into some sort of psychopathology of sexuality.

Bewildered in the extreme, Félicien actually believes that there is a mysterious power out there somewhere, which he must conquer and control in order to convert his Donjuanesque delusion into a reality. When he sets out on his adventure, therefore, he is obstinately chasing that chimera. He first tries that relentless game of posing as an accomplished and totally irresistible ladies' man. Nervously, he tries to prove that in Paris his life was an uninterrupted orgy: "Des maîtresses? Si j'ai eu des maîtresses? C'est bien simple, je ne savais plus où les mettre. On en trouvait dans tous mes placards et jusque derrière le troussequin de mon postillon. Elles craquaient sous mes semelles. Il en tombait dans mes potages" (*Théâtre*, t. II, pp. 16-17). Such is the approach he uses to tempt the young girls whom he accosts as soon as they are far enough from their homes and kin, while doing their wash or taking walks in the nearby hills. The greater the resistance he encounters, the greater the exuberance of his extravagant pose. During a dialogue in the first act, Alice senses that this kind of talk must be fake and tries to warn Mathilde, her companion who appears more vulnerable to the tempter's charms. He answers, "Parler n'est rien. Une seule force compte en ce bas monde. Elle nous ouvre toutes les portes. Elle asservit toutes les rivières. Elle éparpille le caillou des remparts. Elle fait trembler, là-bas, les diables dans les cachettes. Elle détient aussi le secret de l'abaissement des divinités les plus serviables, puisqu'elle est leur mère et leur substance. Cette panacée, cette dynamite, cette fleur, cette douceur, j'en ai tout plein, j'en ai tout plein ma tabatière" (*Ibid.*, pp. 14-15).

But Mathilde is already curious. She wants to learn more about this force. All jokes aside, in her turn, she too wants to believe that that force is real, that it neutralizes all resistance on the part of women and that it ensures for the man who possesses it the submission of an unlimited number of mistresses.

And Félicien's nervousness reaches its peak the moment the two girls walk away. His tension rises, pushing him to delirium. Frustrated, beaten back into his unbearable solitude, he cries out in despair revealing at the same time the preposterous forms of the chimera that haunts him:

Accours, peuple innombrable de mes maîtresses, océan parfumé, soyeux et délicat! . . . Toi, marquise de Chatillon, toute nue dans du velours blanc, toi qui me donnais sur les ongles avec ton éventail de nacre quand je n'hésitais pas à te serrer de près dans le dos du marquis, alors qu'il nous faisait visiter les oubliettes. Et puis, n'en pouvant plus, ma chère, tu m'embrassais tout en marchant, le cou levé, comme une tourterelle qui se gargarisât, et pour que le marquis, alors, marche moins vite, tu le saisis par sa petite épée et tu lui ralentis discrètement le train. Et toi, Marion, la bouquetière, qui me glissais deux pistoles en me cousant une églantine, chaque matin, sur le Pont-Neuf, pendant six mois! Marion! Marion! Vous allez ruiner votre petit fonds! Et vous, madame la Présidente . . . (*Ibid.*, p. 18)

But if Félicien is haunted by eroticism, Mathilde is preyed on by a noble fever of love. For it is love that drives her toward Félicien. It is a mysterious dream, a bewildering paradox. And it is a force that has all the intensity of Félicien's obsession. To her, as a contemplated goal, love represents paradisiac beatitude and heavenly purity. Her next move will be to avoid Alice's watchful attention and to return alone to the place where the tempter lurks. She will then let her soul speak:

Je suis la plus pauvre du village et point, certes la plus futée, ni la mieux polie, mais j'ai noble amour de l'amour. Mon coeur appelle l'amour quand le ciel verdit, là-bas, et qu'une énorme odeur de feuillage et de lait monte de la terre. Les choses, tout d'un coup, marchent plus lentement. La vie se sent si propre et si douce, tellement abreuvée et nourrie de pardon, qu'elle bannit tant qu'elle peut les vitesses qui décomposent et qu'elle assoit l'éternité sur les minutes du bonheur. (*Ibid.*, p. 21)

In the angelic dream she paints with her words, there is not the slightest hint of sensuality. When Félicien tries to kiss her, "to obtain his part of 'terrestrial paradise'," she pushes him back. With the cruel simplicity of innocence she obstinately makes him feel the unmitigated anguish of his problem while unmasking one by one the raw truths of sexuality: "Félicien . . . Quand on s'approche de vous et qu'on éprouve cette odeur prodigieuse, on a horreur, comprenez-vous enfin! Les femmes ont horreur de votre corps, de ce corps douloureux et tendu qui se dessine, qui se révèle, avec une terrible netteté, derrière l'écran vaporeux, à travers le tulle sublime qui fume et flotte autour de vous. Elles ont, du même coup, très grande honte de leur corps" (*Ibid.*, p. 28-29). And in a tone that underlines all the tragedy of this conflict she concludes, "Je vous embrasserai si vous l'ordonnez, mais je vous préviens que mes lèvres seront de pierre" (*Ibid.*, p. 30).

To resolve this conflict, one or the other must be converted. Either Félicien will have to repress his desires and become part of Mathilde's ethereal dream or Mathilde will have to renounce her dream and yield to Félicien's appetites.

Suffering and subsequent death seem to be the immediate results of this confrontation of the two antagonistic tendencies. Mathilde will be slaughtered by the very man who appeared to be the most propitious promise of love. Félicien will be killed almost at the end of a last attempt that seems to promise a solution to his problem also: At the conclusion of the plan, Alice abandons herself in his arms (perhaps the ultimate in irony is shown when, at the last moment, it is Félicien who refuses to make love to Alice).

Eroticism is shown to be an undecipherable puzzle. Beyond the biological aspects, beyond a reflection on the functional role of the glands involved, it awakens a pervasive consciousness of solitude. It is a solitude without remedy. For on the other side of eroticism, the chimerical shadow of love is always present and inviting. As for love, it is the unrealizable dream of an impossible purity. This insatiable drive also results in awakening a consciousness of forlornness which is a more demoralizing form of solitude. For if the frustration of eroticism leads to a consciousness of physical isolation, the impasse of love causes a plunge into metaphysical anguish. In both cases Audiberti seems to stress only the concrete consequence of these drives in real life, which is human suffering. In that respect, in the last analysis, evil is always the winner. Just as "Man of Nature" and "Man of Religion" clash and end up with a triumph of evil, so "Man of Eroticism" and "Man of Love" become docile instruments of evil.

Félicien's case in this juncture has remarkably close affinities with that of Guy-Loup, the hero of *Les Naturels du Bordelais* (1952), first produced by Vitaly in 1953 to inaugurate his new theater, La Bruyère. Like Félicien, Guy-Loup is also obsessed by eroticism. His adventure begins with murders almost like Félicien's: he has strangled to death the young girl who had fallen in love with him.

However, unlike Félicien, Guy-Loup starts as an accomplished, triumphant Don Juan. He actually has the advantage of seeing women falling victim to his charm. He is actually idolized by every woman in the city. In that sense he begins exactly at the point that Félicien aspired to reach. The difference is not all that great, according to Audiberti, for the two obsessions end up being consummated in the same anguish. Guy-Loup lives the same emptiness, experiences the same feeling of perpetual dissatisfaction with himself, as Félicien.

Styled after the fashionable myths generated in the movies, he is considered by all women as an irresistible conqueror. Yet instead of avoiding him, women run after him as though drawn by a frightful, fatal magnetism. Accused of murder, he is acquitted merely as a result of his reputation and popularity. Only minutes after his acquittal, and in order to celebrate his triumph, his hysterical lady admirers gather at the door of the house where he intends to spend the night as a guest of his friend, Dr. Felix Dalbram. Interestingly, in Audiberti's typical situations of allegorical fiction, it is female characters who incarnate "Man of Love." Much more than men, women are possessed with the almost dehumanized dream of a state of love purged of all psychic tension, of all emotional content. The impression often conveyed is that of a state of nirvana, in a paradise of absolute innocence. Thus, Guy-Loup's lady admirers are now infatuated with the charmer as though to confirm that quality of love which knows no limits. In them, the dream of Don Juan's love aims at an act of capitulation in the face of the inevitable and—at the same time—at that mysterious quality by which love is vested with supernatural power. The charmer's magic is shared by every woman who becomes his mistress!

But the charmer's quest is a perpetual anguish. Audiberti's male characters experience it, suffer from it, and speak of it with pathos. We have already seen Félicien's example. Guy-Loup's is just as typical: He is an able, energetic *"libertin"*, but finds himself at the bench of the accused where the public prosecutor demands his head. According to the indictment, the evidence is that he strangled the beautiful and provocative Clotilde. Who is really responsible for this young girl's death? Was she really strangled or did she commit suicide? Thanks to the defense lawyer's eloquence, the defense strategy is successful and Guy-Loup is found not guilty. And that is why evil is meanwhile rampant again. The Clotildes of this world continue to fall victim to a senseless hecatomb. One way or another, the Don Juans of the Guy-Loup variety continue to be the instruments of the bloody rites even if the Clotildes take their own lives, by hanging themselves in their own bathrooms, using a perfumed scarf marked with stamped love mottos, as one of the scenarios in this case seems to suggest.

Guy-Loup puts an end to his anguish by resorting to suicide: He hangs himself in the bathroom with the same scarf he used to strangle his first victim. Once more a grin of irony seals Don Juan's fall: Guy-Loup dies at the moment he is ready to make one more conquest, when Marialène, a young innocent girl, Felix's daughter, offers to capitulate unconditionally and promises her "absolute love" to him.

It is Guy-Loup's confrontation with Marialène that consummates the agony in which the two conflicting tendencies result, as shown in the *dénouement* of the drama. Indeed in this dense, complicated play where the characters' suggestive verbal exchanges help advance true dramatic action more effectively than fast changing situations, the opposition between the two concepts is clearer than in *La Fête noire*. In her way, Marialène follows in Mathilde's footsteps. At first, she is drawn to the seducer by curiosity. With implacable lucidity, in presenting Guy-Loup, Audiberti evokes again all of Félicien's anguish and thus makes the two characters appear as extensions of one another, despite the distance separating their respective points of departure. The demented Don Juanism to which the latter aspires is to the former an everyday lived experience in which he stifles and from which he struggles to escape. The rhetoric he uses to tempt the young girl's innocence is not much different from Félicien's: "J'ai eu quelques femmes mariées, des comédiennes, des dentistes. J'ai même levé une femme du peuple, oui, une espèce de femme de ménage, carrefour de l'Odéon. Elle tenait à la main une miche et des poireaux . . . En général, je fais la jeune fille du monde, de quatorze à dix-huit. Leur bouche sent bon" (*Théâtre*, t. II, p. 235). Both Félicien, the frustrated tempter, and Guy-Loup, the accomplished charmer, fall back into their original solitude, that crushing solitude that Guy-Loup summarizes so tellingly in this observation: "Il n'y a qu'un être, un seul, divisé en plusieurs par milliards. Mais, dans chacun de ces êtres, dans chacun de nous, dure la solitude de l'être général" (*Ibid.*, p. 345).

The tendency of quantitative expansion of eroticism that coexists more or less with the consciousness of its absurdity is also manifest in the case of Maître Lafède in *Les Femmes du Boeuf* (1947), as well as in the case of Madame Cirqué in *La Logeuse* (1954). Both characters' personalities are depicted as dominated by the Don Juan complex.

As was the case with Félicien and Guy-Loup, the myth of an extraordinary force, of a magic of inexhaustible virility is woven around Maître Lafède, the butcher of a Languedoc village. He was nicknamed *"le Boeuf"* because of his corpulence (he weighs one hundred and forty-four kilos) to which his purported virility also seems to be attributed. Married three times, he lost all three wives. But he offered his hospitality to twenty-nine women who now live with him in a harem, in his large, spacious house. As for his dead spouses, they simply could not live with the exuberance of his sexuality. Here is how Madame Gontran, one of his present women, describes the phenomenon during a chat with one of his nieces:

Elles sont mortes de lui, ma fille, et ce n'est pas sa faute, car c'est le meilleur coeur, la tripe la plus sainte. Mais il a le sang trop fort, les humeurs trop vives. Tes deux cuisses, ma jolie, valent à peine son cou. Quand il sort dehors, le soleil se met à transpirer. Il souffle et c'est le vent, c'est le vent sur la mer. Un homme comme ça, si grand que soit son lit, il doit y dormir seul . . . A côté de lui, n'importe quelle femme étoufferait. Il prend tout l'air . . . Tu comprends. . . . ou tu ne comprends pas . . . Il faut l'avoir vu assommer un taureau d'une gifle. (*Théâtre*, t. I, pp. 112-113)

By forming this bizarre harem in his seraglio, Lafède is hoping to accede to the dream of erotic plenitude that he otherwise believes impossible. Not that he is unaware of the precarious nature of this approach. In fact, he is heartbroken when he reflects on his condition. "C'est mon destin. Je me marie et je suis veuf. Je suis plein de femmes et tout seul. Parfois, je pleure . . . Des larmes de boucher, ça ne touche personne, mais, moi, je connais leurs poids (*Ibid.*, p. 117).

But if this palliative that he improvises is not ideal, at least it affords him the possibility of some form of distraction. That is why he suffers a shattering blow when a combination of cirucmstances forces him to face up to a reality he could never otherwise suspect. He discovers that not one of his twenty-nine women had in all this time been faithful to him. What is worse, he discovers that they have betrayed him with his own son! That is why, at the sudden awakening of this alienation, he experiences the utter collapse of his only chance to identify with any destiny he can reasonably consider his. Without his women Lafède has no reason to live.

In a parallel development in the destiny of Lafède's son, we are shown the elaboration of a dream of love. In contrast to the gigantic Languedocian butcher, the son is a puny, feeble, twenty-year-old dreamer. His desire is to get his father's permission to be a shepherd. That desire has been satisfied. Then Lafède has to summon him one day and make him quit his flocks. He believes that at that age his son is ready for the responsibilities of married life and that he needs a wife. Only, in Audiberti's world, things can never be that simple. The son cruelly declares to his father that he does not want to marry an ordinary woman. For his life is now filled with the love he has for a fairy whom he meets at night in the mountains where he lives with his flocks.

Elle n'est pas la même chaque fois. Je la vois, de loin, dans sa robe blanche, qui devient bleue ou noire, selon le jour, ou même verte, avec des coquelicots rouges. Elle s'approche de la masure par de difficiles chemins. Elle lève la main . . . comme ça . . . de tout loin. Moi, je cours devers elle, mais, quand j'arrive, elle s'est envolée dans un bruit de clochettes . . . juste les clochettes du break . . . Et je trouve à l'endroit de ses pieds, quatre fraises sur une feuille de vigne, ou bien trois marguerites comme celles de notre jardin d'ici [. . .] Moi, je me mange les fraises et je me prends les marguerites et je me couche sur la pierre et je m'endors. Mais avant, j'ai posé à côte de moi, un cadeau pour la fée, une rose de source en pierre de couleur. Quand je m'éveille, la rose a disparu. Ça prouve que la fée est revenue. Et j'ai aussi, sur la bouche, un goût de jasmin. Et j'ai, sur les mains, une odeur de poudre, de poudre de riz, et j'ai sur tout le corps . . . (*Ibid.*, pp. 121-22)

Alas, the charm of this experience will not last long. In Audiberti's fiction there is no experience even remotely resembling the occult that does not hide a seed of Satanism. Behind all this poetry, the butcher's son's reverie hides the ugly face of evil. At the end of each encounter the fairy also leaves for the starry-eyed boy a present: a watch, a silver pen, a comb, a powder puff. . . . As he stares at those objects, it is as though an abyss opens up in front of the tragic father, threatening to engulf him: In each of those objects, he recognizes a present he himself on one occasion or another, made to one of his twenty-nine women. All of a sudden he feels robbed of the most precious of his possessions. He suddenly realizes that those women lived at his expense, ate his food, lived off his labor under his roof, but did not belong to him. They lived in a world of their own, a world that excluded him.

But, on his part, the son also experiences an analogous shock, one that shatters his dream of purity in love. Following the final confrontation with his father he still holds on to his dream: "Je suis un berger de montagne avec une fleur dans les dents. Je retournerai sous les astres dans la montagne où tout est pur" (*Ibid.*, p. 127). But it is too late. Lafède will laugh at him. For the revelations that strike the father like thunderbolts also awaken in the son the sad consciousness of a reality he had never suspected: The physical reality of the "human female." The fairy that he was meeting in the mountains suddenly evaporates and, in its place, real flesh and blood womanhood emerges: a hunted, humiliated creature having to betray and be betrayed, caught in a vicious circle, in an inescapable trap. And this way the boy attains maturity and manhood which means that he too finally adheres to, and becomes one with evil. He will follow in his father's footsteps. Will Le Boeuf henceforth have much to look forward to, selling garters in country fairs, as his son suggests? He will reply, "Moi, un jour Lyon et le lendemain Bar-le-Duc, à force de tourner . . . les filles, les rivières . . . c'est en rigolant que je la recevrai, la dernière amazone au rendez-vous de l'homme, la rongeuse de barbaque, la mort" (*Ibid.*, p. 128).

Finally, the obsession with sexual omnipotence seeking to assert itself through a quantitative expansion, as in Lafède, becomes the driving force behind everything that is invention and artful contrivance in *La Logeuse*, a play based on a modern adaptation of the Circean myth. The erotic dream that absorbs Madame Cirqué, the central character, here also leads to a curious craze for possession and domination. Only the case is presented in a somewhat eerier, spookier atmosphere, the message is stated in terms that are more extreme. This modern Circe's appetite is constantly stimulated by an ever increasing energy which finds release in a rapidly growing number of victims, living and dying in terror.

Whereas Lafède adds women to his collection at home under a pretext of goodhearted hospitality, Madame Cirqué serves her obsession with a much less expensive hobby. To satisfy her furious taste for men, she offers the rooms of her large apartment for rent to select boarders enticed by classified advertisements she places in newspapers. As though under the effect of an unknown philter, the men who surround her gradually lose their will, their assertiveness, their dignity and self-respect. She first tries to secure her grip in her own household. From cabinet minister she transformed her husband to a moronic milliner who manufactures silly little hats for non-existent customers. Of her daughter, she has made a pitiful wreck, a neurotic individual who sinks into catatonic depression, who is given to chronic suicide attempts or indulges in outrageous eccentricities. The balance sheet of devastation to which this furor of possession has led includes two dozen more cases of insanity, five deaths, three murders.

Under a heavy camouflage of crackling melodrama, what keeps this woman alive is this insatiable hunger for power over the individuals who can resist her. Men are too weak, too soft, too malleable for her. She is constantly frustrated, living in a milieu inhabited by docile creatures who give in to her, who draw back and are turned into amorphous, flabby blobs. But it seems that one day she does find her match in M. Tienne, one of her tenants. To her, M. Tienne is different from any other man she has known. He seems to have all the virile qualities for which she has a craving. He is strong-willed, intelligent, alert and, above all, aggressive. Soon after she meets him she begins to undergo a transformation herself. It is then that she begins to feel absorbed by a dream of love. An effusion of joy and general well being begins to inundate her. A euphoria until then unknown to her suddenly begins to overwhelm her entire existence which until then, is sinking in the depths of degradation and crime. In the simplicity and spontaneity of her emotions, she is almost like a child.[5] She assembles her victims and announces her miraculous conversion to them. "Je suis conquise, Grégoire, je suis amoureuse. Amoureuse!" (*Théâtre*, t. III, p. 59). She feels regenerated, and for the first time, bathes in the plenitude of womanhood. She proclaims, "Buvez à ma naissance. Une femme vient de naître. Une petite femme. Une gentille femme. Un amour de femme" (*Ibid.*, p. 60).

Could that be a triumph of love? Is the end of the malefic sorcery at last in sight? It seems more like a temporary pause, a precarious truce. For against this reality that expands with bursts of celestial eudemonism clashes the cruelty of another reality, one which is more "real," and which is the permanent one. At the very moment of Madame Cirqué's conversion the tentacles of the omnipresent monster begin to stir. The newly converted witch discovers that Tienne is, in reality, a secret police agent. She learns that he had been planted in her establishment for only one purpose, to obtain tangible evidence of her crimes. In fact, when this man's mission is accomplished, Cirqué is put in prison, her nefarious energy finally neutralized.

It would seem that, at this point, the hegemony of evil would relax its grip. Alas, the sorceress' power emerges again and continues to dominate. Even during her absence, her ghost continues to haunt the tenants. Having regained his political prestige, M. Cirqué is launched into a reform campaign aiming at bringing about changes in the penal code. When his efforts turn out to be successful, one of the results is an amnesty which in one stroke reverses his wife's fortune. The *"Logeuse"* is released from prison and returns to her vast residence where she resumes the deadly tricks of her witchcraft. And by this last development, the *dénouement* suggests rather pointedly that the only perspective possible beyond this point is that of a relentless proliferation of evil.

The works in which we have just traced the depressing dialectic of eroticism and love are samples singled out from among the best known texts of Audiberti's theater. There are, of course, others that would have shown the same thematic orientation and the same overall mythopoeic disposition. As Jeanyves Guérin so justly points out, the references to the Don Juan legend are even more explicit in *L'Armoire classique* and *Bâton et ruban* which are among Audiberti's minor plays. The disconcerting preponderance of evidence is that eroticism and love viewed as the antagonistic impulses that they are in the Audibertian ontology, in themselves and in their correlatives, in their de facto or virtual conflicts, define essential principles of Audiberti's deepseated pessimism.

In the first area of our analysis, the two principles are shown to guide the manifestations of a syndrome. To the extent that the author's conceptual apparatus is consistent with the stylistic devices of his poetry, the syndrome has all the signs of a well-known model identified in our culture in terms of interdicts and transgressions. The syndrome certainly hints at an ancient malaise. But Audiberti's references are difficult to identify. His allusions to the old taboos appear vague and imprecise. His manner of using ancient myths suggests an extensive knowledge of Western mythology. But it is the amorphous and insecure knowledge of the self-taught. Audiberti's intuition into the psychology of transgression, though remarkable, is obviously not that of the Freudian thinking, even if Oedipal connotations and references to the "Law of the Father" are abundant in many of his major plays. But, on the other hand, it is easy to discern as a dominant motif the "funereal ballet" and the "dual song of Eros-Thanatos," as Auzias so astutely points out.[6] The conflict in this instance is an instrument of destruction, of annihilation. It is born of a trauma: a consciousness of the irrelevance or absurdity of interdicts and of the total inevitability of transgression. As this consciousness increases, it tends to stabilize itself in the specter of a cosmic conspiracy (most explicit in *Quoat-Quoat*, *La Fête noire* and *Opéra parlé*).

In this respect, Audiberti's intuitions into the cultural specificity of interdicts and transgressions appear then also to resemble those of Georges Bataille,[7] author of *La Littérature et le mal* and *L'Erotisme*, although it is very unlikely the dramatist had read any of the latter's works extensively.

In our second area the dramatist's attention was shown to divert itself from man's external realities and to focus on different levels of the reality of the self. In the intimate, ever-so-fragile life of the inner self, eroticism and love are revealed to be even more sinister fixations. They are sources of rapidly increasing tensions that sooner or later raise a threat to the psychic unity of the human individual. The character of each is to claim an exclusive and absolute dominion over the self. At some stage, either tendency can invade the reality of the heterosexual human couple (Audiberti's typology does not include homosexuals), degenerate and consummate itself in different degrees of criminal aggressiveness. Such aggressiveness may be directed either against the subject, in suicide, or against another victim, in murder. "The passion of existence" then has no other life to live except the one which will nurture the monster that will devour it. In this scheme of things the sexual being is envisaged as having no other option than to fall from Scylla to Charybdis.

CHAPTER 6

The Impulse for the Abhuman

I *Itineraries of Escape*

WITH regard to the third direction of the Audibertian quest, the exploration is vividly manifest on the anecdotal level in several of his plays and seems to be the generative impulse for a special brand of fiction. Though sketchy, often imprecise and inconsistent, the author's thinking seriously engages on an avenue of speculative projections that aim at a formula to ensure for humankind a universe set apart, where evil no longer will reach it. Step by step, as it becomes crystallized in stages of the creative process, this thinking can be alert and vigorous. In swift glimpses of perfect lucidity it can reach the absolute limit of intelligent reflection, that point where half-truths collapse, contradictions are unmasked, illusions shattered. This does not mean however that Audiberti is gifted with the professional skills of a philosopher. Quite the opposite. He is hopelessly incapable of dealing with abstract concepts. He is also unbelievably inept when he needs to develop a methodical, discursive argument. Though some of his books have the appearances of essays, they consist above all of lyrical outflows, uneven tones and discontinuous rhythms of the uneasy, scattered thoughts of an impatient mind. Such are the texts he published as articles as well as some eight longer ones from *Paroles d'éclaircissement* (1940) to *Les Enfants naturels* (1956), including *L'Ouvre-boîte* (1952) and *L'Abhumanisme* which were meant to be major statements on his personal philosophy.

For Audiberti, any science is of necessity a vain enterprise, since it must rely on human reason. As for reason, he considers it a fatality: "La science, dans ses démarches de détail, s'appuie sur la raison. Or celle-ci, dans quelque sens qu'on la prenne, est la fatalité de l'homme, sa raison d'être" (*L'Abhumanisme*, p. 77). Remaining consistent with that belief, he is totally unconcerned about charges of self-indulgence or self-abandonment in the inebriation of language. Rather than

composing tempered, scholarly manifestoes he proceeds with awe-
some, gigantic strides into a cyclone that lifts up and sweeps away all
the comforting affirmations in which the refined, delicate culture of
Western humanism has so long taken refuge.

By turning his exploration of the problem of evil in this direction,
Audiberti attempts to install human reality into a spiritual landscape.
Under the camouflage of buffoonery, under the mask of ever
exaggerated, dehumanized caricature, the poet's ingenious machines
tick and grind unfailingly. The shocks of demystification they
produce are unoriginal but relentless and efficacious. One by one, they
eliminate all the options open to the rational mind. Amédée, the hero
of *Quoat-Quoat*, exhausts all conceivable means in his effort to
extricate himself from the destiny of the steamship Mirmidon. In the
one act play *Les Patients* (*Théâtre*, t. IV), the same demonic fatality
gradually cancels out the options of the character designated *"Le
Maître à l'oiseau."* In two superimposed worlds, in his store and, on a
larger scale, in his entire kingdom, everything is transformed into a
fuming slaughter house when the war breaks out. In a gesture similar
to that of the Mirmidon's captain, *"Le Maître à l'oiseau"* lifts his
hand, armed with a grenade, and sentences everything to annihilation. Images of similar apocalyptic doom are also evoked in *Opéra du
monde*. A concept of failure appears at the conclusion of the same
reasoning that evidences a hermetically closed universe. A stifling
general ambiance suggests this universe is not meant for mankind.

In the dense, bizarre retorts of Audiberti's dialogues, the recurring,
somber motifs are identified through a proliferation of allusions to
the complexities of the social being, to the fits of passion or to the
conflicts of the religious, political or economic conscience. On the
different planes of the reality evoked by these texts, a biting satire is
often unleashed against the imperfections of the social systems and
social institutions. Thus the message in *Quoat-Quoat* contains,
among other things, an attack against the tyranny of the bureau-
cracies in all forms of collective life. Likewise, *Pucelle* contains a
vehement critique which aims at discrediting the authenticity and real
worth of the great historical figures. In the prologue of that play a
crippled soldier who had his arms amputated, presumably during the
battles inspired by the heroine's visions, profers this bitter indictment:
"Maintenant, limande, ce qu'on se demande c'est si les grandes et
magistrales écritures, Platon, Moïse, elles auraient encore une valeur,
une beauté, dans le désert, dans le silence, là ousqu'y aurait plus
personne de l'humanité pour les lire, pour les écouter. Peut-être tout

simplement qu'elles sont, ces grandes et magistrales écritures, de la concoillotte, de la gangrène de chair humaine arquebusable" (*Théâtre*, t. II, p. 106). A violent satire of the corrupt government administrations also marks *Le Mal court*. The evil of political corruption and dictatorship is openly attacked in *La Poupée*.

In *La Guillotine*, under the guise of facile, overstuffed melodrama, the aims of revolutionary and counter-revolutionary action, Robespierre and the Reign of Terror are similarly under attack. An attack against police brutality and police corruption is also made noticeable in *Le Ouallou* (1956), in *La Logeuse* and in *L'Effet Glapion* (1959). And more than once the Church, the conventional and absurd morality imposed by formal religion, the social norms and the laws of the policed state, the imperatives of secular philosophies are all questioned, refuted, rejected.

Concerning the content of this theater then, despite the author's amoral and nondidactic tone, it serves as grounds for a pitiless indictment of the historical humankind. By saying that evil is humankind itself, Audiberti makes of man a negative value. Indeed all his philosophy begins and ends with this simple formula, namely that human existence is nothing but a dance of shadows: a fleeting and precarious juxtaposition of antithetical principles which cancel each other out. What counts most for the exploration of the problem is what makes possible not only the circulation of evil, but also the consciousness of its grip on man. It is to sum it all up that Audiberti declared, "Sortir de l'homme, c'est tout le problème de l'homme. Mais la question est sans réponse. Celui qui saurait ne penserait pas."[1] Then it becomes evident that, in Audiberti's terms, to "exit from man" is a proposition toward which all arguments stemming from his dialectic of evil progressively converge. It is particularly worth noting that the drive toward the "Abhuman" bears a striking resemblance to the quests made famous through the works of poets, especially Baudelaire, who have experienced the perennial aspiration to transpose humanity in a zone of moral purity, and who have dreamed of "surmounting" the human, as Marcel Raymond so aptly pointed out.[2] It is also worth noting that the temptation to resolve complex metaphysical problems "poetically" is part of a long tradition in French literature. It is perhaps reassuring to observe that at least this tradition remains uninterrupted. Faithful to that combination of Promethianism and Orphism, Audiberti simply takes his turn in confirming once more the poet's right to create the world anew with the powers of his language. He too must elaborate a formula for his part in the alchemy of his literary heritage.

Viewed from that angle, Audiberti's quest must be treated as an artistic exercise which seeks to give expression to the oneiric vision of a separation and of an escape. By the flights of his frantic imagination, this *"Orphée antibois"* applies his talent and genius to translate a message of a radical break. He is often given to easy sensationalism. The effects of his dramatic art are often too uncomfortably allied to cheap melodrama, shallow science fiction and the cinematic "thriller." But he aims high. He is not interested in the passivity or the gratuitousness of these modern distractions. His orientation and theatrical devices reflect rather a practice that became fashionable at the time through the influence of Antonin Artaud.

The rupture proclaimed by Audiberti is based on the same assumptions as the break with the fundamental premises of Western humanism which Artaud had proposed in his manifestoes since 1935. Audiberti's theater reflects the same intellectual posture and the same rhetoric of dissent and protest that we find in Artaud's writings which is a "protestation contre l'idée séparée que l'on fait de la culture, comme s'il y avait la culture d'un côté et la vie de l'autre; et comme si la vraie culture n'était pas un moyen raffiné de comprendre et d'exercer la vie."[3] Likewise, the escape proposed by Audiberti, (such as he suggests it, particularly in his observations on "Abhumanism") is a way of reclaiming for the art of theater the value of the effects of exorcism, incantation and magic—quite in keeping with Artaud's ideas, especially those of his first manifestoes subsequently published under the title "Le Théâtre et la culture."[4] Since the escape consists, for him, in "exiting from man," it becomes necessary that the flights of the imagination toward the "abhumanized" worlds be true eruptions of volcanoes, veritable acts of sorcery, acts of revolt that must tempt the impossible. In a short article he wrote on Artaud, Audiberti even indicates that he considers him no less than a fellow Abhumanist: "Un homme terriblement saisi et obsédé par sa propre humaine réalité qu'il n'accepte pas. Il lutte pour en sortir, sortir de la réalité de l'homme. Devenir chevreuil, archange, nuage ou quoi que ce soit de préférable et d'ultérieur dont nous ignorons le nom et la forme [. . .].[5] It is necessary that the reader be torn off from the comfortable shelter of the foreseeable, the inert and ordered world of habit where history predetermines destiny, action designs the face of the future, the fact shapes the thought, the object announces the idea.

For if evil is everywhere, if it is humankind itself, drama can be born of nothing less than the repeated gesture of provoking the demons guarding the secret behind the servitude and complicity of man.

But the writer who influenced Audiberti's thinking in this area considerably more than Artaud is no doubt Benjamino Joppolo. As Jeanyves Guérin has demonstrated, the Cicilian novelist's *Les Chevaux de bois* (1947) and *Le Chien, le photographe et le tram* (1951) which were published in France in Audiberti's translations, a sort of "nausea of modern civilization" experienced by the characters is associated with the idea of "reforming life" after first destroying its present form. It is more than probable that Audiberti borrowed other concepts as well, more specifically related to this subject, from this friend of over ten years who authored an *Abumanesimo* before Audiberti published his *L'Abhumanisme* (1955).

II *Mutations*

In the poetry that unites patterns of thematic developments and formal devices of style, two main approaches are favored in Audiberti's attempt to give expression to this "exit." One of these approaches reveals the very curious ambition to elaborate a formula of mutation that would actually metamorphose man into another species. The second approach, considerably more developed than the first, involves a tendency to destroy human identity as a conscious reality of the human person. Long before he treats mutation related themes in his theater, the author displays numerous signs of a preoccupation with the physiological realities of the human body, in his narrative fiction and in his essays (cf. *Carnage, Opéra du monde, Les Médecins ne sont pas des plombiers*). These realities, assessed in connection with evil, are in that sense impossible to reconcile with. Mutation then will be a way of doing away with these realities, as is shown in the author's elaboration of fiction. At a moment of extreme tension, in *La Fête noire*, a dialogue between Mathilde and Félicien reveals the meaning of the latter's hopeless pursuit. And that is when Mathilde pronounces the words of apprehension: "Pour que tout aille bien pour vous, il faudrait que vous redeveniez un cerf-volant, un cumulus, que vous perdiez ce caleçon d'os, ce gilet de glandes" (*Théâtre*, t. II, p. 29).

Even for a girl like Mathilde, it is now clear that Félicien cannot dominate women in any other "human" way. It is necessary that, through some process which will start the decomposition of the material complexion of his existence, Félicien must undergo a metamorphosis. He must escape from the physical contour that delineates and delimits him. What magician, what occult power must be invoked so that this miracle can be accomplished? Could medicine play a role? In Audiberti's mind that is essentially the context in which the problem is posed. For we are reminded that both the Bible and evolutional scientific theory support his theory:

L'homme est impliqué dans un cheminement qui l'outrepasse, aussi bien au domaine évolutif animal que sur l'échelle de Jacob. Son espèce est appelée à se transformer, c'est possible, dans ses caractères physiques, cependant que chacun de nous, mort, s'enfile dans une destinée sur quoi tables tournantes et théologies prétendent avoir quelque lueur. Pour l'évolutif animal, c'est aux princes du sang, c'est aux médecins qu'il appartient de concevoir et d'obtenir cette mutation physique, coïncidant à l'évanouïssement curatif de l'être humain tel que nous le subissons. (*Les Médecins ne sont pas des plombiers*, p. 68)

Independently of this vague allusion found in *La Fête noire* and of similar ones found in *Les Médecins ne sont pas des plombiers* (cf. "La Prière du musulman," pp. 29–48), the aspiration to "exit" from the human form by means of a transmutation becomes more precise and more specific in the concluding section of *L'Opéra du monde* as well as in the subsequent adaptation the author composed in collaboration with Marcel Maréchal for a stage version of the same text.[6] In one of the final episodes of this allegorical one-act play, the *"Dominateurs du grand cosmos"* are represented as bizarre creatures from another planet, creatures whose physical makeup resembles that of crickets. Audiberti will expand further on the *"grillon"* theme in *Les Naturels du Bordelais*. In a development of the third act, the dramatist adapts his mythopoeic approach to a fantastic gesture, one that operates a character's metamorphosis much like those of Ionesco's *Rhinoceros*. Nevertheless, the situation here does not involve a sudden attack of an undesirable illness, a terrorizing epidemic like the "rhinoceritis" which threatens to devour Ionesco's characters. On the contrary, the metamorphosis operated here is one by which man's all time dream of escaping man's condition is affirmed as an accessible reality. Pierre Gonfaloni, the great philosopher who was also the tragic Don Juan's mentor, finally becomes aware of the emptiness, the total despair he has helped create. His efforts to create a new world, to build a universe of perfect love, collapse with his disciple's pathetic fiasco, one which teaches him a bitter, almost Camusian lesson on the indifference of man's universe. Disguised as an old woman on crutches, ugly as a scarecrow, this professor of disaster penetrates Marialène's bedroom and makes a final gesture, in an expression of extreme agony, raising his cane toward the wall, "Avec la canne de notre sauveteur j'ai touché hier cette muraille. A présent, muraille ouvre-toi! Que jaillisse pour nous, devant nous ce qui n'est ni la vie ni la mort mais la contrée d'indifférence où la souffrance n'a pas lieu" (*Théâtre*, t. II, p. 292).

It is at that moment that the characters surrounding him start to undergo a stupendous transformation: Gradually, they come to be turned into crickets. Membranous, transparent flaps begin to appear and grow on their shoulders. They no longer have a human voice or heart! When Felix takes his wife's pulse, he verifies a change in the medical data and informs her accordingly. When the radio is turned on, the last testimony of articulated human voice is heard and then the transformation becomes complete: "Paris, Londres, Moscou, Baltimore et Cincinnati sont évacués. Conformément aux vues géniales de Pierre Gonfaloni, les hommes et les femmes se transforment en grillons transparents invulnérables. Dans l'Australie centrale et dans l'Afrique belge on note quelques foyers de résistance qui sont, à l'heure actuelle, en voie de liquidation. Cette émission est la dernière. Le personnel de la radio vous dit glacialement adieu. Kra ta ki . . . Kra ta ka . . . Mi Mi Nia . . . Mi Nia . . ." (*Ibid.*, pp. 294–95).

All the characters are now transformed into crickets, except Marialène. She obstinately clings to her dream of love (which is and remains a human dream). The penalty will prove to be severe: She will be stabbed to death by Pierre Gonfaloni (who finally realizes that his ambitious philosophy is a disastrous failure). Gonfaloni, who can see that he did not succeed in changing humanity as he had hoped, then forces himself on Marialène in order to experience the one thing that he missed all his life, the only pleasure he had to forego, to lend credibility to his messianic calling. When she resists him, he is no longer able to suffer the feeling of emptiness now rapidly growing in him, and kills her in order to eliminate the only obstacle that his insane ambition has ever encountered.

III   *Identity in Otherness*

With regard to the second approach, the "exit" is not so much an "exit" from the human species in terms of change into another species as it is an exit from another abstract reality of limits, the reality of personal identity, this insular zone of consciousness in which our vulnerability to evil is sustained. In the (not so clear) Audibertian ontology, the reality of evil is often represented as constantly threatening to absorb the self. As the self under threat slides toward a reality of deliverance, a sort of "alienation" is taking place. This "alienation" is stabilized at some point through a fission. Indeed the temptation to grapple with the implications of this type of "poetic personality split" is rather frequent in Audiberti's theater since *Quoat-Quoat*. In the case of Amédée, a series of reflections he is forced into following his sentence to death, reveal the nature of the temptation, when he finds himself shut up in a small cabin, face to face with an unintelligent, unrefined *gendarme* assigned to guard him. At one point, Amédée invites the guard to a game in which he pretends to exchange identities with him. But as soon as they begin to communicate from their respective new roles, they find that the experiences they have had in their respective pasts left imprints in their consciousness that were impossible to erase. Despite his naïveté and his general obtuseness, the *gendarme* himself knows how vain Amédée's speculations are: "Il a réponse à tout. Ah! on a raison de le dire, la gendarmerie est une arme d'élite. Ils établissent des rapports du matin au soir, les bougres, et ça serait quoi, l'intelligence, sinon ça, justement, établir des rapports? On peut aussi admettre que l'intelligence se confond avec la sensibilité mais, là, nous tombons dans Condillac" (*Théâtre* I, pp. 52–53).

Amédée's little experiment shows that the prisoner may not easily exchange places with the jailer. Despite the obvious allegorical connotations, the episode was not developed by Audiberti beyond the level of a mere verbal exchange between the two men. But the exploration of the possibilities for this kind of "exit" goes a lot farther in a one-act farce, *Boutique fermée*. A rather minor work, this play is about a beautiful and very virtuous girl who decides to undergo plastic surgery in order to acquire a crushed nose and become, not prettier but uglier. Her motives for this action are saintly: She is so much in love with Marco, a young boxer, that she wants him to lose the inferiority he feels toward her as a result of his own crushed nose. That way he would feel comfortable with her and she would not lose him. But Madeleine's sacrifice on the altar of love will be in vain. Through an ironic twist of fortune, Marco falls victim of an automobile accident. With his face seriously injured, he too must undergo plastic surgery. Acting partly on a motive similar to

Madeleine's, he proceeds to have his nose reshaped. Thus, for Madeleine, plastic surgery ironically became a means of escape from a stifling condition and at the same time a vehicle of doom. While she does succeed in becoming rid of an undesirable identity, she does not accomplish an efficacious exit from the inexorable realities of the human condition, either. For the saintly Madeleine, the problem will remain at the same stage as at the beginning. The same unbridgeable abyss will always stay open between her and Marco.

In another one-act sketch titled *Sa Peau*,[7] the same drive to exit from the stifling reality of an identity animates a pathetic situation in which the psychological dynamics are substantially different from those in *Boutique fermée*, but the basic message is the same. The character tempted with the idea of an exit is here also a woman. A demoralized, glamourless actress in her late forties, one day, in a cabaret discovers Gabrielle, a young singer, timid and unhappy, who shares a physical resemblance with her. Frimoussia takes her under her wing, helps her settle in her room and resolves to live with her by confusing, in her mind, the two human beings. She mixes together in her conscience, two distinct and different realities: the glory she has known as a great artist of years gone by, and the pretty, fresh-looking, alert Gabrielle's young body. In a paroxysm of her obsession, one evening she fires a shot at Gabrielle and kills her instantly in the bed in which they were in the habit of sleeping together.

When the doctor arrives, Frimoussia is in a quasi hallucinatory state, possessed with the insane desire to have Gabrielle's body grafted onto hers. During a last delirious outburst, Frimoussia's tragi-comic babbling reveals the weird nature of the scheme she had conceived and planned to have the doctor help her implement: "Tu me laisseras mon coeur, il tient, le mien, mais tous ces trucs et machins de femme là-dedans, tous frais, tous vifs, mon gars, c'est pour moi, mais dépêche-toi, faut pas que ça refroidisse, ton article, rappelle-toi, l'avant-dernier, le plus conséquent, 'opération doit être tentée dans un délai de quarante minutes après le décès'" (*Les Médecins ne sont pas des plombiers*, pp. 125–26).

As in *Boutique fermée*, the situation presented in *Sa Peau* shows that, at the end of the crisis that culminates in the impulse to "exit" from identity, the escape becomes concrete in this hysteric will to part with the physical envelope of the being, in this fury to "slip" out of the contours, out of the substance of the human body. In the two cases examined above Madeleine and Frimoussia have the same "Abhumanist" urge. Each contemplates the life of another existence

afforded through a material transformation. The existence contemplated by Frimoussia which will result from her fusion with
Gabrielle, will achieve eternal youthful beauty combined with
glamour and artistic glory.

IV   *On the Theme of the Double*

One of the devices that Audiberti uses most frequently in his
dramatic composition is that of the "double." It is another expression
of the Abhumanist impulse, very similar to the "exits" from the
human identity contemplated in plays like *Boutique fermée* and *Sa
Peau*. The characters through whom this aspect of Abhumanistic
escapism is most visible are involved in situations based either on
physical resemblance deliberately exploited in order to seek refuge in
another identity, or in contrived disguise.

The theme of physical resemblance between two individuals seems
to fascinate Audiberti. We find it very frequently in almost every kind
of fiction, in any kind of context. In *Le Cavalier seul* several
characters are presented as having the "same face" (Mirtus's mother,
the Empress of Byzantium and a woman in Jerusalem; the Catholic
priest, the orthodox patriarch and the Ouléma). In *La Poupée*, as we
have seen, the dictator and the revolutionary chosen to assassinate
him have a physical resemblance that eventually makes a substitution
possible. In *Le Victorieux*, the success of the actor Martin Colos in
the role of Cassacata is due to a large extent to his physical
resemblance to the original—which also makes a substitution
possible. In the allegorical treatment of the Joan of Arc myth, a
"personality split" is illustrated by the invention of a second person, a
sister image of the original. But the exploitation of the theme of the
double finds its most fertile application in *La Brigitta*, one of the most
complex and most controversial of Audiberti's plays.

The bold attempt to exit from the asphyxiating area of the personal
self is manifest here, as in *Boutique fermée* and in *Sa Peau*, in a
woman's life. The protagonist is torn between two existences into
which she is driven by the ambitions of two maniacs of cinema, the
seventh art, who exploit her without mercy. In her painful sensibility, the two existences are interpenetrated with such frequency that
she is reduced to an empty shell, a wreck, empty of the slightest trace
of individuality, strangely dehumanized, for her sole function having
to serve as a vehicle to the passions, weaknesses, desires of those who
surround her. From one side, Boisbois wants to "launch" her as a

great movie star. His goal is to draw attention to her. And the man whose attention he struggles to attract most is none other than the great Truffquin(!), a stage director considered the genius of the century. He is successful in launching her, indeed—but into a sordid adventure. He fabricates a publicity gimmick in which the young girl assumes the identity of a certain *"grande dame"* named Pilar Escarcellas, presumably the niece of a South American president. But Boisbois's intrigue begins to backfire as soon as a certain Madame Concourt enters the game. She arrives at the hotel at the time an assassination attempt against Pilar occurs. Surprised by the resemblance between Pilar and the young girl she knew as Paulette Plumard, Concourt too feels she should take advantage of her. Her motive is to give her friend Raoul, a fanatic film director, the once-in-a-lifetime opportunity to make the film of his dreams, the miracle of the century: a superrealistic film entitled "The Life of Paulette Plumard."

Under the pretext of wanting to protect Pilar against her assassins, she proposes that the girl pose for Raoul and subsequently have the film used as an alibi, as proof that the conspirators were mistaken and that the woman they mistook for Pilar was in reality Paulette Plumard. Caught in this sort of trap, Paulette becomes passive, consents to everything and allows things to happen to her. Obtaining effects of raw realism is Raoul's great ambition. To create the proper ambiance for his actress, he takes her to the abandoned residence of the character she is about to play and narrates all her life's "realistic" details to her. In this way, without realizing, he forces the girl again into the cruel reality from which she was trying so desperately to escape and also makes her relive it with twice as much of the pain. Paulette is brutally thrust into a zone of light where she sees herself independently of the image shaped by her defenses. She sees herself the way others see her and describe her when they don't have to wear the mask of propriety or decorum. Here is an example of the image Raoul strives to convey when he guides his actress: "Tu viens de durer trois jours dans une place de dactylo non diplômée. Tu ne trouvais pas la touche des majuscules. Virée, tu t'en vas, droit devant toi, va. Va droit devant toi. (*Jusqu'ici, immobile Paulette marche.*) Tu freines sec. (*Elle ne comprend pas tout de suite.*) Arrête-toi! (*Elle s'arrête et s'immobilise.*) Tu réfléchis sur cette citerne de purée de marrons dans quoi tu te noies sans que tu cries. Bon. Qu'est-ce que nous glanons encore dans la vie? Jamais tué? Jamais barboté? [. . .]" (*Théâtre,* t. V, p. 208).

What torments the young girl most is the fact that Raoul obstinately reminds her that she is limping. In fact, one of the miseries of Paulette Plumard (as presumed by Raoul) is exactly this little defect of a leg that "trots a little less than its sister." But thanks to an operation, the real Paulette had managed to conceal this flaw. So now, under the pretext of making a realistic film, the impassioned director makes her taste all over again the bitterness of a past life she had believed she had left behind forever: Madame Fanny's tyranny, at the seamstress' workshop; the ridicule from the other midinettes, the eccentric, cruel clients; the deceptions and the tears in her love life; the unemployment, the hunger, the illnesses. In a sigh of infinite sadness, she observes, "On me balance. On me vire. On me chasse. En fait, je ne bouge pas. Je ne change pas. Les gens s'en vont de moi parce que justement je ne change pas" (*Ibid.*, p. 222).

For a time, the only escape possible for Paulette seems to be a sort of intrusion into the reality of an object. She turns to the Brigitta, her old motorcycle, abandoned till then in her squalid quarters. Paulette resorts to treating the motorcycle as a human being, as a real companion and as her only friend. In his daring attempt to dramatize the stating of this theme, Audiberti actually presents on the stage the young woman jumping on the motorcycle, "making trips" into different moments of her past and present life. This escape, alas, will be as tenuous as the others. The insane scheme will eventually be undone, when Pilar Escarcellas—the real one—is murdered by her political enemies, an event which forces Paulette into a last and definitive immersion: an immersion into the malignancy that constitutes the life of a persecuted young girl, the life of a futureless, limping *grisette*, permanently inhabited by an impossible dream. In *La Brigitta* Audiberti's statement on the Abhumanistic thesis is made through one of the most sensational attempts at transcending the "oneness" of the self that have ever appeared in contemporary French literature. The epic dimension and the metaphysical implications of the flight attempted by the character in an effort to break with the self constitutes perhaps one of the most poignant illustrations of this intransigent, almost demented, pessimism characteristic of all postwar French theater.

In the creativity that translates the aspirations toward the Ab-human, Audiberti's dialectic of evil which pervades his theater finds the vehicle through which perhaps the entire field of his exploration is covered. The major turning point in the gloomy thinking we have just analyzed occurs in the contemplation of an alchemy. The action of this alchemy is directed to a radical modification of all appearances of "human nature," the bastion of "humanist" ideological orientation. Starting with a reflection on the concept of evil and on the contradictions inherent in the human condition, Audiberti follows basically correct intuitions in attempting to extrapolate problems by increasing tenfold their "resonance." The effectiveness of the solutions he proposes is possible only because it relies on winged horses and flying carpets. Instead of exhausting his resources in exercises of reasoned pessimism which would entail the risk of a static, sterile, paralyzing nihilism, he opts for another aberration: the "deliberate straying" into the calculated immoderation of the *Thousand and One Nights.*

Nearly all of Audiberti's critics have addressed the questions raised by the author's exposés on the concept of Abhumanism. There is no doubt as to the consensus emerging from their assessments. Audiberti's attempt to assert a philosophical posture in the form of a coherent doctrine has been inconsequential. His arguments in *"Guéridons abhumains" (Age d'or,* No. 3, 1946, pp. 33–34), his dialogues with Camille Bryen in the *"Colloque abhumaniste," L'Ouvre-boîte,* his articles in *La Parisienne* (later published in a volume titled *L'Abhumanisme*), as well as a variety of related statements in his *Entretiens* with Charbonnier and in other interviews have certainly led to no conversions.

What does Abhumanism mean exactly? "C'est l'homme acceptant de perdre de vue qu'il est le centre de l'univers" (*L'Abhumanisme,* p. 35), proclaims Audiberti. It proposes a subdued state of consciousness: "Amoindrir le sentiment de notre éminence, de notre prépondérance et de notre excellence afin de restreindre, du même coup, la gravité sacrilège et la vénéneuse cuisson des injures et des souffrances que nous subissons." And if no practical benefit is derived from such a consciousness, if humankind remains unable to "abolish evil," at least Abhumanism will have taught us to take refuge in a haven affordable by the riches of language: "nous aurons du moins dû mettre à profit le jeu des mots, l'espace libre, ou vide, entre les objets vocabulaires, pour exprimer que nous détestons toute doctrine, toute drogue . . ." (*Ibid.*). It is more than a cross-breeding of materialism and scepticism, more than a "stoic's marble bust in a naturalist's locomotive." "Disons qu'il enfonce des portes ouvertes," is Audiberti's answer to his own questions.

Michel Giroud, an ardent Audiberti admirer himself, will not hesitate to state, "Il ne résoud pas le dualisme qui l'habite; il ne l'affirme pas, il ne le nie pas; dans ce sens Audiberti n'appartient à aucune tendance philosophique précise [. . .] Tous ses essais sont des impressions sans suite où il change sans arrêt de sujet; [. . .] Sa pensée n'est jamais discursive, organisée, défendue, étayée par de solides arguments et par une logique sans faille; . . ."[8] Jeanyves Guérin's assessments are more or less of the same tenor: "L'éclectisme et le nihilisme s'appelant réciproquement, voilà qui rendrait compte des innombrables citations d'auteurs, convocations de doctrines et compilations de systèmes qui alourdissent les articles et ouvrages d'Audiberti, comme *Les Essais* de Montaigne."[9] In the same vein, in his *Hygiène des lettres*, Etiemble addresses the dramatist as a "vieux compagnon de route," but regarding the Abhumanist thesis, he has nothing but scepticism to express: "Si l'abhumanisme se bornait à renvoyer dos à dos Sartre et Maurras, Drieu et Zola [. . .] qui ne serait votre allié?"[10] But Audiberti himself did not seem to have any illusion either about his skills as an essayist or about the impact of his rhetoric on Abhumanism, as some of his avowals show: "L'Abhumanisme échoue. Sourire, ils me font sourire les deux bouquins où j'essayai de cimenter, consistante, une doctrine de l'homme . . . L'Abhumanisme finalement, ne signifie à peu près rien" (*"Rouge," N.R.F.*, Dec. 1960).

In a most thorough and in-depth study of the literary manifestations of the Audibertian abhumanism, in 1976, Jeanyves Guérin demonstrates more than convincingly that whatever other name the author might have given his brand of thinking, the *"métamorphoses abhumaines"* may not be interpreted either as a closed system or as an answer to the impasse that the pessimism of Samuel Beckett's generation has had to come to grips with.

L'ère des dryades est révolue. Les idées de transmutation, de sublimation, de métamorphose ne sont pas susceptibles de réalisation ici-bas. La société, l'histoire, la science, le progrès condamnent le projet abhumaniste, alchimiste ou baroque, d'évasion radicale. Ce n'est que dans le rêve ou dans la surcréation esthétique que l'homme peut échapper à sa finitude d'être englué dans l'immanence materielle. Il ne peut y avoir non plus de régression vers un en-deçà édénique, vers l'innocence perdue, ou, en d'autres termes, de retour à l'état présocial de nature.[11]

It is perhaps precisely for that reason that the bursting lyrical exuberance of Jacques Audiberti's works continues to intrigue. For if the admirer of Jiordano Bruno[12] and Benjamino Joppolo is unsuccessful in offering some hope of "doctrinal recuperation," or some kind of tomb for all conflicts and contradictions inherent in classicism and traditional humanism, he puts all his faith in the inexhaustible vitality of language, a vitality he himself often has had to rediscover or regenerate. With the intuition of a great visionary, he declares himself on the side of the true revolutionaries of his era: Dali, Miro, Picasso, Braque. With the fixation of the "Abhuman," Audiberti does not engage in a futile, frivolous exercise of self-indulgence. He offers literature the "tin can opener" of an optimistic solution (cf. *L'Ouvre-boîte* where the image is explained as an instrument of survival). During the postwar period, when his theater appears on the Parisian scene, literature goes through a limbo of systematic doubt. Man is depicted as a hunted animal, morally destitute, stripped of all the old certitudes as to the values he should pursue, as to the tasks he should undertake. Life being envisaged as totally empty of meaning, heroism in the traditional sense is a mere platitude or a laughable absurdity. No feat of virtue can be found justified, no transcendence justifiable. A literature that claims Existentialist credentials painstakingly illustrates the superfluity of existence and heralds its dreary message by means of a dry, anemic rhetoric. In the wake of the "absurd" consciousness, a passion of negativism subverts the heretofore unquestioned notion of dignity attached to the writer's vocation. Only shortly afterward, the subversion will expand with a view to discrediting the nobility of the act of writing itself. It is in that context that the Audibertian literary venture must be assessed. And it is in that context that it asserts itself by reminding the author's contemporaries that the *Word* is still sovereign and omnipotent.

CHAPTER 7

Structures of the Abhumanist Message

I *The Accidental vs. the Essential*

SINCE the time of the first performance of *Quoat-Quoat* in 1946, the critics covering Parisian theaters for the press have rarely missed an opportunity to point to this intriguing talent of the dramatist from the South by which he was generating unmistakable effects of black humor by mixing irreverent Ubuesque truculence and Claudelian incantatory symbolism. But this does not mean that it extended open arms to him. Audiberti was not saluted as a new luminary of the postwar, leftist or *"engagé"* literature or of any other kind of avant-garde. There was at the time what Jacques Lemarchand used to call *"la petite presse"* which adopted a negative attitude toward the drama of this bizarre newcomer. Those were extremely difficult times for the Left Bank theatrical avant-garde in general. As it happened with Ionesco, Beckett, Ghelderode and others, the author's plays were produced in minuscule, uncomfortable theaters and for a public often limited to a dozen spectators drawn mostly by curiosity. The avant-garde of the poetic theater which, at the time, included authors like Pichette, Schéhadé, Ghelderode, Vauthier, shared the same fortune as the so-called "Theater of the Absurd." The unfavorable press reviews often reflected a narrowmindedness and hostility which were out of all proportion and surely undeserved.

It is somewhat ironic that in Audiberti's case the criticism dealt mostly with the author's use of language. Audiberti's works were routinely disparaged for lack of discipline in composition, as well as for lack of purposeful restraint in the use of vocabulary. It is also significant that approving or praising assessments were not infrequent, dealing with that same aspect of the author's works. In such assessments, Audiberti's exercise of poetic language was represented

112

as conveying a message of genuine renewal. Here is a typical example of this kind of conflicting value judgment. On the occasion of the first production of *La Brigitta*, Jean-Jacques Gauthier, theater review columnist for *Le Figaro*, wrote: "L'histoire est inintelligible. Produit d'une logorrhée délirante, il entasse des boniments de camelots, des plaisanteries dont rougirait l'Almanach Vermot, des dialogues incohérents; il aligne des mots sans suite où la grossièreté le dispute à une démence qui doit être fausse puisqu'elle n'a pas la logique de la vraie; jargon, baragouin, charabia, comment qualifier ce style qui ne veut qu'épater à grands coups de calembours détestables ou d'allitérations insanes."[1]

On the other hand, in a review of the same production, in *Le Figaro Littéraire*, Jacques Lemarchand had this to say:

Il [Audiberti] fait de ce langage une charge délirante, où se mêlent—mais allez donc les démêler parmi tant de bruits!—les trouvailles personnelles les plus admirables et les jeux de mots, allitérations et contrepèteries les plus triviales . . . Et derrière tout cela il y a encore une histoire gentiment mélodramatique dont une motocyclette au coeur sensible et à la réplique nette est l'héroïne.

La Brigitta est une surprise, même dans l'oeuvre d'Audiberti qui n'est faite que de surprises. Elle contient beaucoup plus de choses et de traits et d'inventions que le public, dont je suis, ne peut en recevoir en une seule soirée, quand il n'est pas averti . . .[2]

In those two examples of contradictory judgments we find a reflection of the two basic attitudes that determined the positions of the press regarding the author's theater at that time. What some considered weaknesses or aberrations, in a sort of controversy developing as the number of judgments multiplied, others viewed as richness, originality and therefore evidence of strength and worth. The polarization at that point was simply reaffirming ambiguities and contradictions of previous assessments: "Verbiage incohérent . . . bavardage insupportable . . . dialogue décousu," were the terms of the implacable verdict of Jean-Michel Renaitour.[3] In contrast, the judgment of Pierre Marcabru on the same subject was, "Cette langue est d'une richesse extraordinaire, d'une richesse spontanée, non point le résultat de l'avarice et de l'usure, mais au contraire née de la dissipation de tout un patrimoine de bavard, et cela avec une prodigalité de grand seigneur."[4]

Some prestigious names figure on both sides of the controversy. Under the aegis of Gauthier, the negative point of view was developing into an almost reactionary intransigence, summarily rejecting Audiberti's excessive license with syntax and vocabulary as a shock to common sense and good taste, even as an affront to public morality. Henri Gouhier, Robert Kemp and André Billy sided more or less with that point of view. Among Audiberti's admirers and his champions were Jean Paulhan, Boris Vian, Guy Dumur, Georges Lerminier and especially Jacques Lemarchand, author of the largest number of review articles on Audiberti's theater written by any one critic on either side of the controversy. The debate eventually embraced a wider range of questions, going beyond the strictly literary stylistics of drama, beyond the problematics of intelligibility of written texts transformed into stage productions. Critics often raised some of the technical questions dealing with the art of live spectacle in general, particularly with the perennial question of the "theatricality," of the poetic image enunciated exclusively by live speech (cf. Poirot Delpech's article in *Le Monde*, Sept. 7, 1962).

But it is now indisputable that a gradual change in attitudes was taking place, as more and more of the author's texts were exposed to the public, especially through successive publications of his drama in book form. By 1955 the climate was ready for a final conversion, as the revival of *Le Mal court* showed. What contributed most to the rediscovery of that play was neither a change in the author's style, nor a revision of the original plot. For this was the same text that had been used for the production of nine years ago. The director who happened to be the same also, the actors who were also the same in the 1955 production as in that of 1947, the public and the observers of the press, had all changed their attitudes. As Audiberti's plays continued to gain support through exposure on the stage, the barking of the "little press" subsided. The review columnists' rhetoric lost the venom of the first invectives. Less shrill-voiced, more competent judges were now being heard. It was being discovered gradually that the apparent disorder in the constitition of the Audibertian text was evidence of a conscious, intentional, mastered system of esthetics. That, if the author sacrificed the "essential" to the "accidental," it was worth finding out why, in his case, the "accidental" was almost always superior to the "essential," as Kléber Haedens observed, in 1963.[5] A good deal more categorical in his assessment of 1967, Michel Giroud wrote, "Nous affirmons que l'oeuvre d'Audiberti n'est pas obscure ni cahotique ou disparate si l'on veut l'aimer et la comprendre; elle possède au contraire, malgré son abondance, sa diversité, sa plural-ité, une unité remarquable [. . .]"[6] Likewise, in 1974, Jean-Marie

Auzias would also dismiss the charge of incoherence by defining the Audibertian formalism and general inspiration in terms of the author's affinities with the Baroque. Obscurity and incoherence, according to Auzias, are only apparent to the French critics who are generally of a Cartesian, Classical bent of mind. In a reference to the Parisian critics' reactions to *Le Mal court* he observed,

Il va de soi que la critique, française, cartésienne comme il sied à Paris, s'y est généralement trompée et a foncé comme un seul homme sur la plus française, la moins occitane des pièces de notre écrivain, *Le Mal court*. Il va de soi que toujours malherbienne et vaugelée, la critique n'a même pas entrevu le baroquisme de cette pièce classique qui est faite pour un petit décor à la Sans-souci de Potsdam. [. . .] La logique des personnages déconcerte l'esprit étroit du français cultivé qui ne voit qu'incohérence là où, bien au contraire, triomphe la cohésion baroque d'une architecture en perpetuelle fuite.[7]

Understandably, Audiberti himself had rejected this charge rather categorically, as his statements in the *Entretiens* with Charbonnier indicatė: "Je ne comprends pas pourquoi on me taxe sans cesse d'intempérance verbale, voire de 'logomachie,' alors que quand j'écris je n'ai vraiment d'autre soin et d'autre souci que d'employer les mots les plus exacts, en m'efforçant de les faire coïncider avec ce que je peux avoir de pensée . . . Pourquoi me taxe-t-on de magie verbale?" (*Entretiens*, p. 85).

Viewed in its entirety, the universe of Audibertian drama has often been described as a mirage. In each work the poetic flight that the author employs as a device of escape is renewing the attempt for the pressing displacement of the Abhumanist search. The reality Audiberti proposes to abandon is the reality that enters into a bond of complicity with evil. It is the reality of the unresolved conflicts, the reality lived in the tragic consciousness of an impasse. In that respect, it is obvious that any kind of mirage could be the best conceivable practical achievement that could be attributed to the ambitious aspiration toward Abhumanism, given the failures of the author's discursive essays.

One day, critics of the psychoanalytical school of thought will no doubt complete a definitive account of the dynamic field of a fictional psyche that can be reached through the author's works. Meanwhile, the "mirage" will remain a relevant metaphor for a qualified, specific account of Audibertian escapism. Several of the author's well-informed critics seem to concur. Pierre-Aimé Touchard refers to the zones where the author's flights seem to be drawn as *"mirages avoués,"* and finds them characteristic of a trend represented by many other dramatists of recognized talent (Marcel Aymé, Ghelderode, Schéhadé, Genet). Others have associated the Audibertian escapism with a spiritual quest of biblical references, a quest aspiring for a restoration of Eden. The latter point of view is reflected particularly in assessments offered by Alfred Cismaru, Paul Surer, and George Wellwarth. The three seem to share the view that Audiberti tends to identify Eden with a primitive state of nature, with a world termed "pagan," and "Dionysiac."[8] But the mirage metaphor is adequate only to a limited extent. In Audiberti's case, the Abhumanist thesis is too complex to be totally accommodated by an image like mirage.

To fully understand the message of the Audibertian literary work, one must grasp the forces at play in the process of writing, affecting the entire field. The most pertinent way of addressing this problem would be focusing on the norms of specificity in the functioning of his medium itself and studying the generative dynamics of his text. For even though the term Abhumanism never became the all inclusive metaphor of a major philosophy, the Abhumanist impulse we analyzed in the preceding chapter has always been a real force. As such, it is a fact that it dominated every aspect of the Audibertian production. For that reason, the value of defining the relations between the generative process and a thesis enunciated in terms of a pure abstraction of negativity is self-evident.

We can study the nature of Audiberti's Abhumanist passion first as antihumanism in the historical/cultural sense of that term; in other words, as an attitude toward a literary past and a literary heritage in terms of ascribed values. On the level of the writer's medium, we find that to be apparent in the choices he makes for his personal mythology, in the choices he makes for a referential framework on which fiction is built. But we also find it apparent and, in a most interesting fashion, in the author's elaboration of a special idiom, of an "idiolect" which asserts itself as a reflection on, and a critique of, established values in the sociolinguistics of the French literary culture. Thus the Abhumanist, antihumanist message asserts itself as a subversive manifesto, attacking something basic and well-entrenched.

A generalized critique of humanism is by no means Audiberti's exclusive predilection. The poet from Antibes is the product of a literary milieu that has been shaped by several antihumanist messages. PostRomantic French literature has been in a continuous crisis of self-denial, in a continuous "crisis of self-destruction," as a perceptive poet observed, the year of Audiberti's death.[9] Lautréamont, Artaud, the Surrealist theoreticians, Robbe-Grillet and the analysts of the *"Nouveau Roman,"* all assume antihumanist postures, promoting an "Abhumanist" persuasion of one kind or another. Audiberti's posture is not altogether original against that kind of background. In his *L'Abhumanisme* where he attempts to specify the system of values he proposes to attack, the "enemy" is carefully identified, although one may disagree as to the accuracy of the data alluded to as facts. It is the humanism of the era known as *"le grand siècle"* and of whatever elements of it survived and prevailed in what the author calls *"l'humanisme boulevardier."*

II   Codes of Abhumanist Fictions

In the preceding chapter we surveyed the themes and thematic dispositions used in Audiberti's dramas, in a way revealing the Abhumanist impulse and the Abhumanist message. On a somewhat more "formalistic" level, we can now survey the impact of the Abhumanist concepts as they become operative postulations exactly where the "generative laws" governing the production of the Audibertian text are most directly affected. In fact we find that we can survey a distinct typology of procedures the effect of which we propose to call "regressive modulation," by analogy to similar processes in the plastic arts, and in proportion to the author's Abhumanist postulations. Here is how it manifests itself in the constitution of the text.

In the author's choices of exuberantly assertive, lively settings and unforgettably bizarre human characters in works of fiction, the "regressive modulation" is first noticeable in a consistent retreat into historical time, in a backward movement in "chronological" time as registered by the calendar. We have seen that Audiberti has a predilection for evoking a picturesque décor of past eras of human history. In strictly statistical terms, we notice that the anecdotal content of sixteen out of twenty-eight plays is situated in periods other than the twentieth century.[10]

By placing the action of his plays in past eras, Audiberti is not merely adhering to the familiar rule of Classical literary tradition where "remoteness" in time is pursued in order to enhance the paradigmatic character or the timelessness of certain themes. Neither is he attempting to "update" old myths and perform a function of demystification as seen in the works of many of his contemporaries (cf. Giraudoux, Anouilh, Sartre, Camus *et al.*). It is not at all an attempt to reconstruct old myths in order to establish new relations between distant moments in history. As we have pointed out in a preceding chapter, what is most often found in Audiberti's recasting of the past is an almost naturalistic reconstruction of a geographic and psychological reality. It is depicted with relish and with an obvious taste for an unharnessed proliferation of detail defying the most fundamental laws of economy of language in composition.

By this movement in the generative process, the regressive conditioning promotes fantastic frescoes suggesting by their contours and by their ever changing tints the overabundance of life in a locale bearing the marks of a bygone era. It is a movement that adapts the text so as to convey the rustic atmosphere, the bucolic or primitive colors of countryside. It is reflected in the choice of characters, in that special "mythical" quality of their portraits. It is also reflected in a multilevel depreciation of the individual human being through esthetic adjustments of the characters' speech styles and through adjustments of their "visual" dimensions. There is a unique modulation of the social, political and moral content of the human persona presented on the stage. The characters are enveloped by a veil intended to accentuate the bizarre, indeterminate simplicity of the primitive, the innocuousness of the rural naïveté, of bucolic candor. Their dialogues evoke the delightful flavor of dialectal speech identifying well-known sociolinguistic zones of the French provincial scene, or suggestive of analogous environments in imaginary regions. Characters like Lou Desterrat, Madame Palustre, Toulouse, Jeannette, the soldier Hennoi, the soldier Bégore are typical examples.

But the movement of the regressive modulation is not apparent only at that level. Its action is corrosive. It proceeds to the point of twisting, deforming, distorting. The utterances of these characters tend to degenerate to parodies or burlesque pastiches of their literary antecedents. And it is at that level that the Abhumanist character of the modulation is perceived most unambiguously.

Here are some examples. Addressing Félicien, Lou Desterrat describes one of the victims of the beast of Gévaudan in these terms: "La pauvrette, par bonheur, n'a plus besoin qu'on la guérisse. Elle porte, dans le blanc du cou, la marque profonde de dix griffes de fer qui se sont rejointes et touchées. Nous ferons, s'il le faut, la Révolution, mais nous posséderons la bête coupable. Nous l'escagasserons et la clavellerons" (*Théâtre* t. II, p. 33). Jeannette and

Joannine, discussing the latter's imminent conversion, have this exchange:

> Jeannette. —Quoi ça veut dire, une apparence? Une dame blanche?
> Joannine. —Oui. Et toi, ta coiffe, tes sabots, tu n'es toi-même qu'une apparence.
> Jeannette. —Pour une apparence, entre nous soye dit, je paraissions pas beaucoup. Mais c'est-i normal, dis-moi, c'est-i régulier qu'une unique personne elle se distribue en deux tout en demeurant la même?
> Joannine. —Le fils du Seigneur du monde est bien à la fois là-haut dans la joie, et ici, sur la croix. Mais c'est difficile à saisir.
> Jeannette. —Attends voir. Je sommes toi. Je sommes toi chaque fois que tes beaux amis sont point là pour t'a regarder. Je sommes la fille de cette maison agricole et paroissiale. Je sommes toi. (*Théâtre* t. II, p. 153)

In *Bâton et ruban* almost the entire text is a dialogue between Vauban and his secretary. The illustrious Marshall of France, Commissioner of Fortifications, spends the last moments of his life dictating his will to his secretary Ragot. At the doorstep gather the dying veteran's mistresses, women of local stock whose bizarre jargon presumably is the patois of the region. As they chatter, sounds resembling the lyrics of a folksong and coming from a distance outside draw their attention. But the words forged by the author for the occasion are, as the stage-directions indicate, deliberately "confused," intended to convey only the "resonance" of Languedoc parlance:

> Doù grand Sèbas
> é dé sa rodo
> plén li douï bas
> é la quibrodo
> m'én venguéri guéri guéri
> . . . .
>
> (*Théâtre* t. V, p. 145)

In the second part of *La Fourmi dans le corps*, the sly Marie Mathias, one of the "ants" at Remiremont, starts an animated conversation with the coadjutrix. She is asked to return her illegitimate child to Barthélémy who earned the right to motherhood by preventing the destruction of the Abbey. But Marie Mathias is not about to give up her baby. Frustrated as she may seem, she is far from helpless. Her devious mind will soon flirt with the idea of a ruse. And instead of her charming little boy, the basket she will finally prepare for Barthélémy

will contain Ratatinot, the idiotic, slobbering dwarf. Her peculiarly
colorful speech is typical of the fabricated slang that Audiberti cultivates in pursuit of his special effects.

—Jamais, Madame! Jamais! (*Revenant vers le lit, à l'invisible enfant.*) Ah!
Elle veut un moutatiou! Ce n'est pas toi que je vais lui donner, vu tout ce
grand sabbat qu'elle fait pour t-avoir chopé dans ses draps, que moi, chiure,
j' t'y ai mis! (*Lors on perçoit la voix récitative de l'enfant, cependant que
les rideaux du lit remuent comme si, derrière, il dansait:*) Le roi doré, n'a
qu'un papo pour y loger tout son troupeau, rapipi, rapipo, rapinette, rapipi,
rapipo . . .
—Chut, mon chéri! Doucement! Lui désordonne pas son plumard, cette
chichemaille de l'entonnoir, la sale rapiate qui dérobe sans pitié! Tu vas t'en
revenir à la maison, chez nous. (*De la main elle calme l'agitation des rideaux.*)
Mais il faut que j'en déniche un autre. Sinon, pas moyen . . . (*Elle se saisit de
la hotte.*) Un autre à mettre dans la hotte . . . Un autre, qui veuille bien . . .
(*Elle ouvre la porte, sans toutefois sortir. Aussitôt pénètre la rumeur vocale
de l'escalier:*) va-t-en chez les bergers!—Montre-nous ta jolie voix!—Chante,
Ratatinot! Chante! . . . (*Théâtre* t. IV, pp. 188–89)

In this general type of modulation then the characters are
developed with a technique that subverts the polished, civilized,
refined and intellectually advanced or complex in favor of the
backward, rough, uncivilized, primitive. In a more specific way, and
in a much more emphatic manifestation of the "regressive conditioning," we find the technique particularly effective in the
treatment of prestigious historical figures. Vauban is depicted as a
frivolous, almost clownish, old chap, as a gross womanizer with
earthy manners and an overall peasant idiosyncrasy. The glorified,
prestigious Vauban of the legend, the admired builder of ports, canals
and aqueducts, is hardly sketched in the background. The same can
be said of the emperor Diocletian in *Le Soldat Dioclès*, of Joan of
Arc in *Pucelle*, of Turenne in *La Fourmi dans le corps*. The historical
importance of these legendary figures is deliberately diminished by
the depreciative action of the regressive conditioning. Their existences are envisaged by the dramatist in understated, devalued,
simplified décor; their gestures are caught in their spontaneous,
instinctive motions. They are stripped of all conscious motivation
that would justify the meaning that was conferred on them by history,
in a hierarchical order of values.

Nowhere is the "devaluation" more impressive than in the
stylization of speech styles. Audiberti has left us no ambiguities on

this subject. As he explains in *Dimanche m'attend*, in the fabricated idioms spoken by his characters the depreciative function is served by two jargons. For the colorful patois he attributes to his peasants, he uses the term *"l'argot du bonhomme."* But an analogous jargon is clearly noticeable in his plays based on twentieth century settings and situations, a sort of fabricated *"argot parisien."* In the author's perception, this jargon is in many ways a pariah language. It is repressed, pushed aside, excluded from "good company," in sum, a language that exists as an adversary of prestigious formal French, the jargon Audiberti likes to call *"ce français de Paris, royal, impérial ou présidentiel."* It is the jargon that bursts and proliferates practically everywhere in the author's work evoking contemporary life. It is the *"langue verte,"* the idiom Audiberti calls *"dialecte abhumaniste"* (*L'Abhumanisme*, p. 57).

Here are a few typical examples. In *La Logeuse*, a young police inspector announces that Christa's fiancé *"a cravaté la reinette."* To help understand the expression, his colleague volunteers a translation: "il a dévalisé la caisse." The same inspector will continue with similar statements in fake Parisian argot: "Le mironton a mis le cap, tout fumant, sur l'écurie de la pépée. On va jardiner un peu partout dans la chaumière. Et puis, surtout pas de jérémie, pas de rébecca. Nous avons le fantômas avec toute la paraphine voulue. *Il brandit un papier"* (*Théâtre* t. III, p. 52). And the same colleague again will offer to help. Turning to Madame Cirqué he will explain, "Pour une fois, je ne sais pas ce qui leur a pris, pour une fois, nous avons un mandat. (*Il prend le mandat d'arrêt que lui passe le jeune inspecteur. Madame Cirqué s'en empare.*) C'est ce qu'il voulait dire quand il disait le fantômas, étant donné que le papier c'est comme les fantômes, c'est blanc" (*Ibid.*).

In *Le Ouallou*, the action is situated in the basement of the police headquarters. Glinglin-les-Dormantes, the much-feared archcriminal who is one of the detainees, can force his bold demands on everyone. His language style is nothing but a clever pastiche of the argot usually identified as that of the Parisian underworld. Here is how he addresses the *"Gouverneur de la sécurité,"* when he needs the latter's help in ensuring the theft of a valuable painting:

Le radjah de l'Oklahoma m'a commandé le *Débarquement*. Il m'a câblé mardi dernier. Si on chloffe de trop, il vérolera. Pour nousailles, fils! cent grosses briques, sec, dans le gant, sans déboutonner. A quoi ça te sert, de gouverneur la Sécurité, si tu es pas bon de décrocher un chromo dans un corridor? . . . (*Ibid.*, p. 180)

In *Pomme, Pomme, Pomme*, the plot is based on a parody of the Adam and Eve story. Audiberti uses the entire range of his familiar tricks to create his equally familiar theatrical effects: disguises, hidden identities, prestidigitators' tricks and the like.

In a situation of allegorical farce, Dadou and Vevette, ridiculous couple of the Audibertian Sixteenth Arrondissement variety, go through a sequence of adventures that illustrate the author's somewhat ambiguous critique of the inscrutability, ambiguity and cruelty of the designs that the creator may have regarding mankind. But while the themes and the situations may be banal, the verbal fireworks dominating the long dialogues are full of entertaining surprises. Here is a sample of *"argot parisien"* in the diction of Zozo, the prestidigitator, who uses the image of a fruitfly to create a metaphor of Vevette/Eve: "Regardez-moi ces pattes de mouche à rotule inversable, ces ailes que leur minceur apparente à la surface même de la lumière, et cette charnière génitale, regardez! regardez! dix-huit membranes, de quoi souscrire une épée d'honneur au fier moucheron qui la mouchera" (*Théâtre* t. V, p. 26). Toward the end of the second and last act, the same Zozo, cracking a whip, will take a dim view of Dadou's laziness: "Je vois le genre. Monsieur tire au cul. Avis! Les ramiers, nous les descendons. Les cailloux, nous les cassons. Numérote tes chromosomes, foutu muscadin! (*Il pousse Dadou devant le récipient aux déchets.*) Cette boîte de vitesse, là tu vas me la faire briller comme la prunelle du sultan Mahmoud. Allez! Frotte!" (*Ibid.*, p. 97).

Another manifestation of regressive conditioning is highly visible in Audiberti's stylizations of "inner" experience of time, in the consciousness of fictional characters, lived in terms of continuity or discontinuity. Without being directly connected with Abhumanism, the techniques employed in *L'Ampelour*, the author's very first play, mark a significant preoccupation with the question of the "alchemy," and more specifically, with the question of the anteriority of language in our perception of reality or the question of reality perceived as a condition of language. In this play, a clearly defined movement of "regression" in time is triggered in the consciousness of a group of peasants going through a hallucinatory experience, in the lounge of an inn, in the Massif Central area. At first their small talk is insignificant, boringly trivial. But, little by little, a mysterious tension begins to build, triggered by certain words. In an inexplicable atmosphere of bewitchment, the words pronounced by these simple-minded languedocean peasants enter into a game of irresistible verbal associations which are nonetheless without any conceivable relevance to the subject of their conversation: "Toutes les eaux de la montagne sont pleines d'ombres. Qu'est-ce à dire? Elles sont, ces ombres, plus noires que la moustache des gendarmes ou que le lacet de soulier des vieilles qui vont à la messe. Elles dénoncent les oiseaux qui nous viennent depuis un mois par les châtaigniers d'Ovinage. Mauvais présages" (*Théâtre*, t. I, p. 84). In the animated exchange that follows, from one allusion to another, the structure of a complex allegorical drama emerges. From a discussion of birds, the conversation almost inexplicably moves on to an order of symbolic representations dominated by the image of the *eagle*, which eventually joins an associational scheme where the images are further adjusted to evoke specific memories of the Napoleonic campaign. In this freewheeling verbal exercise, the alibi seems to be a parapsychological phenomenon presumably caused by a real event: the death of Napoleon Bonaparte in Saint Helena, in 1821.

An atmosphere of expectation is created in that inn. From time to time the innkeeper would slip out on the pretext that he heard footsteps of someone approaching the door. During this suspenseful period, there are three knocks on the door. Each time a new character is introduced into the lounge: first a priest, then a butcher, then a blind man. When a fourth knock is heard, it is a messenger announcing, "Messieurs, l'empereur Napoléon vient de mourir à Sainte Hélène, là-bas. Le télégraphe optique vient de nous annoncer que l'empereur Napoléon est mort à Sainte Hélène" (*Ibid.*, p. 107).

The familiar, reassuring order of causes and effects has been reversed. Through this nightmare, the reality relived by the Languedocian peasants is not the reality of an event taking place in the present—in this instance, Napoleon's death in 1821. What they do relive with heightened intensity is an experience they went through six years earlier—the traumatic moment of Napoleon's return from Elba. By the procedure employed in *L'Ampelour*, Audiberti appears to assert the belief that the historical time of an experience such as the emperor's return from Elba can be restored entirely and assume all the authenticity attributable to an experience lived as present through the miraculous, demiurgic powers of language which is the only authentic reality. His views must have been reinforced later when, in fact, in *La Nouvelle Origine*, he asserts that language is the beginning of every reality and the true origin of the cosmos, "L'histoire est immobile, parcourue par des générations séculaires. L'histoire est une géographie, une territorialité, marquée de points fixes, Catherine

de Médicis, Wagram, l'incendie de Rome, Ugolin et ses enfants, le
poète Fortuna, où tour à tour, séjournaient des êtres, des objets, des
incidents repassant, selon des intervales honnêtement reproductifs,
aux mêmes endroits d'une circonstance publique . . ." (*La Nouvelle
Origine*, p. 9). And a little further, he adds, "Nous allons essayer de
présenter, de mettre au présent toutes les présences" (*Ibid.*, p. 11).

Since *L'Ampelour*, Audiberti did not give us evidence of any
interest in the dramatic genre till 1945 when he wrote *La Fête noire*.
But from then on his techniques have been in constant evolution. The
regressive conditioning gradually developed and matured as it
became more consistent with the author's evolution toward the
antihumanist positions he assumed in the 1950's. In his approach to
expressing the reality of time and the experience of continuity, the
same type of modulation of his devices is visible in many of his plays,
notably in *Le Cavalier seul*, in *La Brigitta* and most of all in *L'Effet
Glapion*. In the latter, the orchestration of multiple, heterogeneous
literary devices makes the effect of regressive conditioning on the
entire work visible in an almost exemplary fashion. For here the
modulation integrates the widest variety of stylized but dated esthetic
elements with the most remarkable degree of consistency: pastiches
of stock situation comedy routines, effects borrowed from the oldest
and most banal theatrical traditions, from the farce, from melodrama, from vaudeville. The interweaving of all these elements
becomes a source of continuous surprise and a process that reinforces
comic effects that otherwise would have been mediocre.

Without being the author's best play, *L'Effet Glapion* constitutes
the most typical example of Audiberti's success in his unclassifiable,
personal art of collages which amplifies the theatrical experience
through a dizzying juxtaposition of pastiches. In his preface to the
1959 edition of his play, the author explains the premises of this
approach by suggesting that his play is a new type of Vaudeville,
modified to suit the cultural realities of a postSurrealist era and to
stress the need for defining values in esthetics: " . . . le moment vient,
un certain périple achevé, de rêver devant le pur objet d'art, tel qu'on
en trouve dans les bazars de souvenirs parisiens, cygne en porcelain
ou vase mauve fileté d'or, n'importe quel truc en cristal condamné à
vue d'oeil par le bon goût, mais qui nous reposât enfin de nos
systèmes mal assurés et de nos rêves confus" (*L'Effet Glapion*, p. 11).

Whether it is a modernized vaudeville, as the author wants it, a
vaudeville *"surréalisant"* as it was termed by the critics of the 1950's,
or a *"divertissement baroque sur les aventures du Réel,"* as suggested

by Jeanyves Guérin, the play was a remarkable box office success and made everybody happy for several seasons at La Bruyère.

In the first act, we are apprised of the meaning of the title as well as of the main theme of the play: "l'effet Glapion, décrit pour la première fois par le professeur Emile Glapion, consiste dans l'usufruit d'une donnée concrète objective par la logique visionnaire subjective" (*Ibid.*, p. 56). By all appearances, the play claims to illustrate, as the subtitle, *"parapsychomédie"* suggests, a parapsychological type of events and in the opening scene we risk taking everything a bit too seriously. Luckily, the comic art of Audiberti's *furor eloquendi* soon transfers us onto a terrain where we are awaited by the benumbing, uninterrupted shocks of high powered, pure entertainment.

The plot takes its initial impetus from a situation which is by any criterion entirely plain and unassuming. On a Sunday afternoon, Blaise Agrichant, a physician, his wife Monique and a captain of the constabulary, their guest, are at table near the end of their dinner. There is no sign of anything unusual, much less of any tension between these old friends spending a quiet Sunday afternoon together. Then slowly, a bizarre transformation begins to take place. In Monique's mind, the little ritual of this otherwise trivial dinner party in the presence of her husband and the old friend, triggers a series of transpositions through which she gradually drifts into another reality. Subsequently she reaches the reality of another time framework and begins to relive the reality of another Sunday afternoon, a significant Sunday afternoon experienced exactly one year ago. On that day, Monique was not married to Blaise. She was instead his assistant, in love with him but very unsure of his intentions. As for the captain, he had been courting her for some time. That afternoon Blaise had gone hunting and Monique, alone in the house, was receiving the captain who had come for a brief visit, but decided to take advantage of the doctor's absence to finally try to seduce his young nurse. Also, that afternoon, when the doctor returned, she received from him at last the proposal of marriage which she had, with very little hope, been expecting for a long time.

Against this kind of psychological background, Audiberti sets out to represent what goes through the young woman's mind at this commemorative moment which is a major turning point in her life. In a very rapid succession of scenes reminiscent of cinematic narrative techniques, a veritable cascade of theatrical effects follows, animated by interspersed explosions of unrestrained buffoonery. But while we are distracted by this profusion of pranks, *quid pro quo*, disguises, transformations of characters and Ubuesque adventure, we gradually become aware of the one thing the author aims at above all else, and which is to make visible "the secret and continuous life of the human mind." The transition is blunted by the sustained movement of regression commanding instantaneous passages from the present to the past. The seesaw motion between the reality of the present and the recaptured reality of another moment a year ago has the effect of unveiling, stirring and liberating underlying strata of psychic life: fears, fleeting illusions, repressed desires, disparate reveries and the like, of the kind expected at the conclusion of a psychoanalyst's therapy session.

The unfolding of action assumes its liveliest pace in dialogues like the following between Monique and one of the doctor's clients:

Cliente, *accent provincial particulariste.* —Quel affreux temps! Le ciel bleu, le soleil! Quand il pleut, mes rhumatismes, je me dis, c'est la pluie. Mais sitôt qu'il fait beau, comme aujourd'hui, plus moyen de s'en raconter. Je me les ai. Je me les regarderai. Les rhumatiques cherchent le coeur. Tant qu'ils ne touchent pas le coeur, vous allez, vous venez. Les gens ne se doutent pas ce que vous endurez. [. . .] Et les médecins! J'en ai fait, allez! J'en ai fait. (*Montrant le bureau.*) Celui-là? Comment s'appelle-t-il, déjà? La mémoire, moi! . . .

Monique. —Agrichant.

Cliente. —Agrichant.

Monique. —Le docteur Blaise Agrichant.

Cliente. —Agrichant ou pas, c'est un spécialiste. Il prend combien?

Monique, *toujours impressionnée.* Combien? Combien il prend? Deux mille, je crois.

Cliente. —Il va me faire déshabiller, je les connais, tout enlever de A jusqu'à Z et Z jusqu'à I grec, même ma peau de chat [. . .] (*Ibid.*, pp. 66-67)

Before long a stupendous extravaganza begins. The lady client takes off her clothes, presumably to be examined by the nurse; but behind those clothes suddenly the old woman disappears. What appears underneath is a burglar, the formidable villain Gilly. The purpose of his visit is the doctor's safe. Transformations of this type, abrupt identity changes, sleights of hand as in a continuous magician's show fill the atmosphere with an effervescence of gargantuan proportions. The same effervescence dominates the verbal exchange such as this explosion of oratory occurring when Monique delivers a speech on behalf of a princess in one of the final fireworks, toward the end of the play: "Sa phosphorescence qui s'accroche aux idoles de droit divin, elle entoure également ces poupées sans particule ni généalogie, les étoiles de l'écran, les comètes du plateau. Triomphez, mes petites! Triomphez! Votre gloire ne passera que trop tôt. C'est vous, les femmes proprement dites, vous les épouses qui faites les cuivres, le potage, les enfants, le parquet. Vous en régalez-vous comme il convient, de la sphérique intimité rectangulaire d'une cuisine, loin des dangereuses guirlandes de mandarines nocturnes de Broadway, Hambourg, Changhaï, San Remo?" (*Ibid.*, pp. 161-63). When the last fireworks are extinguished Audiberti underlines the conclusion of these rites by bringing everything back to the situation opening the play, with the familiar tableau: Monique, the captain and Blaise having just finished their dinner.

In both *L'Ampelour* and *L'Effet Glapion*, the texts attaining the status of literature are constructed by the backward movement toward a reality that must be retrieved bit by bit from the deep recesses of a zone of consciousness that can be *real* only in language. It is not an attempt to recapture time past in a new glory as in Proust, where the present is a necessary bath that enriches, amplifies and "sweetens" a privileged moment of the past. The regressive conditioning aims at seizing a moment where time is at point zero, where history is no more. Audiberti's Abhumanism is *"le monde sans l'homme,"* as Michel Butor has only recently reminded us.[11] Jeanyves Guérin also made this pointed observation, "par sa dérision anti-hegelienne d'un absolu historique, il annonce le nihilisme politique de l'antithéâtre."[12]

III   *Codes of an Abhumanist Grammar*

Finally, the regressive conditioning manifests itself on the linguistic level in a way that determines not simply an "idiolect" based on jargons corresponding to sociocultural castes but the "performance" level of the author's medium in terms of intelligibility or general functional effectiveness. It is at this level that the translation of the Abhumanist theses into a process of language transformation is the most subtle and the most interesting.

The author's critics have all signaled this aspect of the Abhumanist philosophy aspiring to become a metaphor of a system of esthetics or a metaphor of a formalistic approach to literature (in the Mallarmean sense or in the sense of a literature preoccupied primarily with its own form). "Sa langue comme sa pensée est abhumaniste: c'est là surtout que se manifeste son désir de sortir de la prison langagière habituelle, officielle, contemporaine; son goût de la mutation s'exprime claire- ment dans son langage [. . .]," wrote Michel Giroud.[13] Ten years earlier, in his excellent study of the author's *"Théâtre en liberté,"* Guy Dumur had written, "La tentation est grande en lui de mettre en question ce langage qu'il aurait peut-être voulu d'oc [. . .]"[14] About the same time, underlining the depreciative function, Dominique Fer- nandez wrote: "Audiberti, [. . .] gonfle le langage dans une explo- sion baroque de sons pittoresques et bizarres, afin de mieux l'abaisser."[15] And as recently as two years ago Jeanyves Guérin wrote, "Le dramaturge utilise la matière phonique des mots pour faire communiquer ses personnages, mais de surcroît il prend un malin plaisir à rompre les conformismes lexicaux et phonétiques, en multipliant les intrusions hétéroclites et les écarts stylistiques le point commun des dialectalismes, des argotismes, des mots étrangers, des sabirs et des néologismes consiste dans une déviation inattendue par rapport à la norme usuelle."[16] But more specifically, Guérin also sees in the author's use of language the processes that translate the Abhumanist message, although he is more interested in studying links with "preclassical" literary idioms that might relate Abhumanist esthetics with the literary baroque.[17]

Audiberti's literary posture, the authenticity of his art, the technical specificity of his personal "style," can stand on the merit of these "contaminations" of language that perturb the time honored models of performance, that spoil the game we have grown accus- tomed to expect inside the "literary" text.[18] For these deviations are symmetrical and complimentary to the conditioning of the referential frameworks we examined above, in the conscious or unconscious choices involved in the constitutive structures of fiction.

In that respect he is not quite without affinities with the theoreti- cians of the narrative of the 1960's who, in the more extreme of their tendencies, subvert the notion of "masterpiece" and finally the notion of literature itself, retaining only the concept of "text," or *"écriture,"* limited to designate only the work of an author/scribe.

The "regressive" function is served at this level through a variety of procedures, uniformly motivated toward a generalized "deflation." Here are some examples.

A strange, at first incomprehensible, tendency visible particularly in the author's theater is the one to produce, in the progress of a character's speech, pseudo-vocables presumably belonging to foreign tongues. The overall effect may be the immediate comic charge of parody or a sense of the bizarre suggested by a vague, purely phonetic sort of exoticism conveyed by vocal sounds which, in themselves, are certainly nonlinguistic emissions. The diction of Joannine, the future Joan of Arc, was perverted by a language alluded to as *oungrien*, according to her mother who underscores her discovery by mimicking her daughter's speech: "Spoumaviana tchitchifof bougougou." Soon we are told that the girl mingles with soldiers who pass through the countryside and "catches" their cursed language like a disease. According to her father, "Quand ce n'est pas le oungrien, c'est le luxembourgeoisiau. Chaque soldat qui passe déteint sur elle un peu" (*Théâtre* t. II, p. 119). When it becomes clear that Alarica's wedding with *Roi Parfait* will not take place, the disenchanted would-be bride sings a song especially composed for her wedding, in Courtelande, in her own national language: "Sti via préchouiss ta ngarok/Dra nagocène polista/Dak amour sbinvidie miarok/Fala roui mi sta . . ." (*Théâtre*, t. I, p. 159). Jacques Coeur addresses the slave of a Beyrouth merchant in the latter's language, presumably Arabic: "Barca, Selim! Lazem t'ergach fel baladak. Mouch momken te Khaliak héna Samheni" (*Théâtre*, t. IV, p. 41). In *Le Cavalier seul*, in Constantinople, capital of the Byzantine Empire, a choir blasts out Orthodox liturgical chants, presumably in Byzantine Greek: "Karoïphas, Karoïphas. Hinémoun élison ofa. Karoïphas . . . Karoïphas . . . Aspaloff hibrinos inoum (borborygme) brrou'ha" (*Le Cavalier seul*, p. 158). And in the following scene in a Jerusalem street, a Mameluc, a piper and a veiled old woman converse in Arabic:

—Kroum frama franoum abala larrla n'h'roum.
—Akemena schalla bdala.
—Akra stlla m'Kazenet effen rahnet palta viz stella brrouz . . .

(Ibid., p. 163–64)

In *L'Effet Glapion*, Frombellded escorts princess Augusta to the Agrichants' residence and at the threshhold pronounces words that are supposed to be in the princess' national language: "Hiss, Boisgnegge. Chaugor. Chtillon. Druff. Comsou press . . ." (*L'Effet Glapion*, p. 189). And in *La Brigitta* Boisbois pronounces words meant to be Chinese, in a statement that Madam Concourt disdainfully appraises as a "Mandchou proverb": "Ghoum phar sfok noum pioupioupiou bonifoum zamak" (*Théâtre*, t. V, p. 246). Equally as ostensible in the Audibertian text is the regressive conditioning manifest in the author's much talked about "verbal inventions" both in terms of coined word vocabulary and in terms of syntactic patterns. The transformations of reference models is overwhelmingly consistent with the Abhumanist theses, as Jeanyves Guérin's analysis of the author's word derivation norms has shown. The author of *Le Théâtre d'Audiberti et le baroque* lucidly appraises the motivational factors and the stylistic impact of lexical archaïsms, regressive modifications of words, borrowed terms from technological and scientific lexicons, folk neologisms.

Without going too deeply into the technical problems of the author's "Abhumanist grammar," we can see clearly to what extent the different modes of derivation tend to contribute to the uniformity of certain effects or of certain types of expressiveness. In suffixal derivation, the morphology indicates a preponderance of pejorative and diminutive morphemes, as Guérin points out, such as -asse, -asser (*tièdasse, crapulasse, paysannasse, mignonasse, frottasser, embrouillasser*), -aille, -ailler (*nonaille, gendarmaille, mahométaille, traficailler, chantonnailler*), -ouille, ouiller (*tramblouille, démange ouille, escribouiller, écornouiller*), -et, -ette (*pouponet, sapinet, tripette, nouvelette, faribolette, bambinette*). Also, in suffixal derivation, we find the tendency to transform into "folksy" vocabulary through more complex processes: *drolichaille, frelucaillon, crottonillette, foutrefouillette*. In other modes of derivation, we find combinations of heterogeneous morphemes parodying the original "respectable" models: *fourmisophie, paillosophie, cacaomane, homorastie, laryngito-philosophie, movietoner*. We also find derivations involving heterogeneous elements parodying scientific vocabulary: *plurimétrique, phosphatiné, carbogazeux, hydroporphyre, architonerre, intellectronique, mirlitonaire, mesméroscope*. In all instances, the coined word is a deviation from the idiom that we know as "cultivated" French. Audiberti does not expand his vocabulary for the purpose of "enrichment," in the same sense as the Pléiade, for example. Very appropriately, Jeanyves Guérin rectified a major misconception when he noted in his conclusion, "la dilatation du vocabulaire audibertien provient essentiellement des emprunts et des calques . . . et secondairement de la production néologique, donc de l'imagination linguistique du poète."[19] And that is a capital point, in every consideration of Audiberti's verbal exuberance. Abundance in Audiberti is a vehicle to a special type of message. *Deformation* is distinguished from invention. Entirely original inventions are few in number in the Audibertian vocabulary.

As for "verbal inventions" in syntactic patterns, the modulation most often visible is one that cultivates structures having their own laws, belonging to a rhetoric of depreciation. The patterns resulting from this modulation are integrated in discourse through the speech of characters, and their effects are aimed at promoting a succession of little crises, constantly renewed, of the articulated, rationally ordered systems in which "literarity" in the French historical context is fixed. The preponderance of comic effects often produced from such modulation, are directed against the same targets. But the patterns of this category are otherwise irreducible. They are *Audibertisms*. As those who knew the dramatist personally often observed, Audiberti wrote as he spoke. That is, no doubt, part of his personal mark of genius. Henri Mondor gave perhaps the most accurate assessment of the author's professional idiosyncracy when he wrote: "Jamais improvisation moins douteuse, spontanéité, moins surveillée, richesse aussi prodigue . . . Sa fougue, son impétuosité, restent éloquentes et l'éloquence, quelque volubilité qu'elle s'accorde, quelques trésors verbaux qu'elle entraine, se donne imperceptiblement le temps des idées inédites et des rythmes inventés."[20]

Audiberti's is indeed an eloquence that builds on the ruins of the system of rhetoric it demolishes. It undermines the classical compositional norms, notably the ones governed by the requirement of *"clôture."* The explosive, digressive tirades of Madame Palustre, Guy-Loup, Madame de Concourt, Dadou . . . are open affronts to the classical code of basics: order, propriety and decorum, coherent reasoning, economy and concision of language. The impact may be quite forceful, as, for instance, in the ramblings of Madame de Concourt in *La Brigitta*:

> Chez une jeune fille blonde éprise de chateaubriands, de chateaubriands et de tournedos, les résidus solides pèsent davantage, en plus foncé, notez-le, que le crottin bouton d'or d'une négresse paradoxalement gavée de cacahuettes. Donc mangeons léger. Mieux, ne mangeons plus! Laissons notre boyau tripier se ratatiner, s'évanouir . . . Remplaçons-le par du muscle compact. Pour accélérer le crépuscule du côlon le laboratoire que je commandite mit au point trois substances alimentaires de base, la farine de gousse de chrysanthème, la salive d'abeille et la queue de souris déshydratée du Japon. Elles agissent à travers la peau, directement. (*Théâtre*, t. V, pp. 228-29)

Similar looseness in the compositional schemes of equally long tirades abound in most of the author's plays and result in texts that seem to be constituted like growths of the "biological" and "vegetal" orders rather than under the control of a conscious, rational intelligence, as critics have often pointed out.

Apart from the long, digressive tirade which in itself is a pattern resulting from the "regressive conditioning," with a distinct stylistic character, and making of seemingly unmotivated massiveness or abundance an assertive, anticlassical statement, "verbal invention" is also manifest as a type of modulation interfering with the order of prose discourse in terms of special effects of resonance and rhythm normally reserved for the formal contours of poems. Thus the dialogues are often interspersed with statements such as, "Nous disposons d'assez de serge et de coton pour les munir de mamelles et de jupons" (*La Fourmi dans le corps*). The type of syntactic structure where the choice of an assonance and a rhythm arrangement appears to assume such prominence is extraordinarily abundant in the author's theater: "C'est à force de l'attendre que je déflore les enfants. Et d'aiguille en aiguille, j'étrangle ma famille" (*Opéra parlé*). "L'homme et la femme issus d'un rêve sans second, debout sur leur domaine insultent le dragon. M'attire en toi ma forme en partie étrangère qui me creuse une chair plus dense, plus légère" (*Pomme, Pomme, Pomme*). And elsewhere in the same play, "Adieu, petit monde où ne surabonde que l'atrocité! Adieu, le théâtre où l'on doit se battre pour être cité!"

In another category of structures which are also abundant, Audiberti seems to expose the ambiguities of pure grammaticality in the order of discourse that remains rational but ignores the phonetic realities of language: "Marcelle. —Quand tu dis Saint-Pourçain je comprends cinq pour cent" (*Coeur à cuire*). Elsewhere, "Madame Ferrobrett. —Un loup vous mord. Vous êtes mort. Cercueil. Si vous êtes blessé par un sanglier les emplâtres vous sauveront. Cerfeuil" (*Le Soldat Dioclès*). And in another play, "Vevette. —Depuis que je suis mariée j'aspire à ce que possède toute femme civilisée, un aspirateur" (*Pomme, Pomme, Pomme*).

In yet another category of patterns corresponding to striking rhetorical figures, we discern the same conditioning in the play of fabricated metaphors and locutions: "Water" becomes *"la femme du feu,"* or *"la mère des alcools."* We also find the same conditioning in the deflating effects achieved by pejorative locutions aimed at the specialized discourses of modern technologies and sciences: *"Le cinéma pyramidal en tralalacolor," "style buteur taciturne à mazut comprimé," "boîte de vitesses de bolide cosmonaval," "tubes nécro-gènes fulgurants silencieux."*

And finally we detect the same conditioning in syntactic patterns in which an impeccable grammaticality is sustained only to enhance the effects of what appear to be "disoriented" or "wayward" proverbs, enlisted nevertheless to serve the same rhetoric of derision: "au solstice d'été l'oeuf noir grossit avec la lune," or "les lacs du soir naissent des glaciers du matin," or "à joie sans fin succède fin sans joie," "Planque en Suisse, le diable te le rendra," or "quand l'animal commence à refroidir les moustiques font place au vautour," or "un bon tiens vaut mieux que deux tu l'as-z-eu."

As far as the author's attitude toward language is concerned then, despite obvious affinities, Audiberti's indictment of humanism falls short of the vehemence of Artaud's humorless message. Audiberti does not seem prepared to commit intellectual suicide in order to establish contact with the depths of primeval sources. Neither is Abhumanism on par with the relentless thoroughness of Céline's invectives, shaking the foundations of the Western conscience. In a somewhat strange way, it seems more akin to the posture of the man of letters such as assumed by Raymond Queneau. The latter's tendency to view the creative process as a game, to consider the specificity of literature as inseparable from a type of "demolition" and perpetual "recycling," differs very little if at all from Audiberti's adherence to a principle of regressive conditioning.

To conform with Audiberti's Abhumanist esthetics, literary vision and literary language must be kept alive by constantly looking back. But the author's concept of regression is not a reflection of simplistic conservatism. Just as the concept applies in the plastic arts, regression in Audiberti is more related to a movement from one style to another. And yet it sustains a persistent character of aggression. It is not recuperated. As it governs the constitution of the author's work, it combats every kind of conformism, at every level of the process. It is difficult to measure the extent to which Audiberti consciously remains on his guard, ready to attack and subvert. But he is clearly in solidarity with the pioneers of modern theoretical reflection on the nature of writing and the tenuous systems of values it involves. His practice of regressive and depreciative, modulation techniques does not constitute a sterile, absurd exercise in nihilism. And yet it would be impossible to conclude that the transfer of Abhumanist theses to the operative levels of the literary process can be reduced to a mere attempt at enrichment and renewal. In his own

inimitable way, Audiberti is worthy of the most ambitious architects
of narrative theories and explorers of narrative techniques of his time
(cf. Maurice Blanchot, Jean-Pierre Faye, Philippe Sollers *et al.*) As is
the case with almost every one of them, he came to the realization that
the place for literature cannot be other than the heart of that
supreme ambivalence: the process of language. For Audiberti has
learned, as have the most lucid of his contemporaries, that there is
only one way for language to accede to the privileged state of
literature, and that is by accepting existence in the uncomfortable
axiological limbo maintained by a perpetual state of transitivity.

CHAPTER 8

Conclusion

I *On the Author's Milieu and his Values*

FORMULATING value judgments on Audiberti's total production is not an easy task. The author's mentality and temperament shown in the preceding chapters, as well as the preponderance of the depreciative reflexes attested to by the Abhumanist posture would tend to make ordinary means of rating literary values rather inadequate. Time and again, the author's critics who attempted to offer totalizing appraisals, or those who articulated comprehensive conclusions as to the worth of the Audibertian literary accomplishments, have found that labels such as Baroque, Classical, Romantic, NeoRomantic, Symbolist, Surrealist and the like, convenient as they are, may also become aberrations, if applied without caution. While they may be relevent to one or another aspect of a single work, they become meaningless when used to characterize a tendency reflected on the author's entire production. By and large, the degree of complexity and the polysemic nature of the Audibertian literary statements elude all labels. We become aware that no valoristic assertion can be useful unless we succeed first in assessing the precise confines of relevancy within which the Stranger from Occitania, the poet of the Empire and the Retreat, the inscrutable novelist-narrator-scriptor of an endless tale, and the dramatist of the Abhumanist gospel can be viewed as specific, communicative identities on *their own* terms. It is only then that we can attempt to define what we may reasonably deduce as a meaningful legacy this author's works can be expected to pass on to posterity.

In terms of the milieu and the cultural background which formed him, Audiberti seems to be a peculiar mixture. His personal religion is untouched by the Catholic environment in which he grew up. He is knowledgeable of, and profoundly impressed by, extraneous religious elements such as the rituals of the Catholic Church. Yet in terms

135

of personal faith, he confesses that he is a nonbeliever (cf. *Dimanche m'attend*, p. 41). We cannot help but notice in his attitudes a profusely, sumptuously expressed mysticism. But it is distinct from any type of personal need for spiritual nourishment. It is almost a paradox that his obsession with religious themes, his fascination with religious symbolism, his awareness of Christianity as a major force in the West are all assimilated in him in such a manner that he can respond to creative urges with a remarkable critical detachment. And when he does reveal his choices in terms of values, his attitudes are colored by an almost romantic nostalgia. Paganism always comes out more respectable than Christianity. A diffuse notion of pantheism, probably inspired by Giordano Bruno, his Abhumanist hero, is also reflected widely both in his dramas and in his essays.

The poet from Occitania is a Mediterranean, as has often been pointed out. But the appellation can be misleading. It is indeed little more than a reference to a stereotype. His idiosyncracy, his talents and skills do reflect the values of Latin culture to a certain extent (his exuberance, his lyricism, his bent for treating words as objects, or as individuals, his bent for manipulating poetic images, meter, rhyme). His liking for the Judaic history, traditions and cultural values is also well pronounced. As Mandiargues pointed out, "dans le Juif il chérissait l'individu par excellence, le support de la souffrance et du succès, ces deux pôles humains dont il ressentait l'attrait comme la fascination." Nevertheless, we have also had more than one occasion to observe how alien he is to Greek values. This is particularly true in what Mandiargues has so accurately termed "sa méfiance ou son inaptitude à l'endroit de la construction logique et généralement de ce que l'on appelle philosophie."[1] And it hardly need be stressed that the poet will remain the Stranger from Occitania throughout his life: He will remain conscious of his native land as being apart from the consecrated images of French national identity. He will retain a consciousness of its distinct regional culture, its mores, its religious history since Charles Martel and the Battle of Poitiers (cf. *Le Retour du Calife*, p. 1) and since the days of the Cathars and of the Albigensian Crusade. He will retain a strong emotional attachment for the regional linguistic heritage.

For the novelist, the same values seem to be reflected in the works of narrative fiction. As Henry Amer noticed in 1956, the author's novelistic characters are not merely incarnated. They also "belong to a country, to a province, to a town: They were born either in Antibes or in Paris."[2] As for the dramatist, Audiberti's values must also be considered in that context, as well as in the terms of an additional element: his exposure to and influences by artists such as painters, and people from the theatrical world, actors, actresses, directors. This crowd of friends and acquaintances with whom he associated at various times of his life included some influential figures of the Parisian artistic community: the painters Leonor Fini, Hugo Cléis, Jean Carzou, Camille Bryen; the actresses Suzanne Flon, Catherine Toth, Françoise Vatel, Catherine Milinaire; the directors André Reybaz, Jean Le Poulain, Marcel Maréchal, Jacques Baratier and, above all, Georges Vitaly. Since Audiberti's death, several of these personalities have published their memoirs in which we are presented with revealing accounts of the author's dealings in his private life.[3]

Similarly his values must also be considered in terms of his exposure to cinema, to the numerous films he viewed and analyzed in his review articles, in which we can see to what extent he has been influenced by the art of directors like Max Ophuls and Baratier. His circle of friends and acquaintances also included known playwrights of the theatrical avant-garde on the Left Bank (Adamov, Ionesco, Schéhadé, *et al.*). It is debatable though whether any of them, with the possible exception of Eugene Ionesco, may have exercised any influence on him. Unimpressed by his contemporaries, Audiberti had distinct predilections for playwrights of the past. Unique is the example of Molière on whom he wrote an essay, at the invitation of Jean Duvignaud, the historian of contemporary theater. Alas, it was a disappointment to Molière scholars as Audiberti chose to deal with aspects of Molière's private life rather than his dramaturgy.

Adding then all these factors to the major literary influences which we underlined on various occasions in the preceding chapters should help account for all that Audiberti may have acquired directly or indirectly from his milieu in terms of values and perhaps even tastes. It is in this wider context then that we should evaluate the author's accomplishments and particularly his own system of values as it is reflected in his Abhumanist credo.

II *Values and Counter-Values in Abhumanism*

The critics of Audiberti who dealt persistently with what they perceived as his defects reproached him essentially for his unwilling-ness to make an effort on behalf of, or his inability to conform with, the conventions and established practices of the civilized Western milieu in which he expected to find a public for his message. To a considerable extent, this criticism is understandable and valid. Even today, to the author's seasoned fans and to neophytes alike, the Audibertian text is a difficult terrain to penetrate, and reading and understanding it remains a very demanding task. In this respect, it is obvious that relevance and proper perspective are of the utmost importance. The problem is a modern one but by no means does it concern Audiberti alone. The issue of "readability" was debated extensively, and often heatedly, in the 1960's in connection with some tendencies of the so-called *Nouveau Roman*. And however unsolvable these controversies may have been, it was realized then that it is impractical, wasteful and even aberrant to rate the worth of a "literary" work merely in terms of the size of its readership, or in terms of the degree of difficulty it poses for its readers. The lesson learned then applied just as much to Claude Simon, to Michel Butor and to Robert Pinget as it did to Philippe Sollers and to Jean-Pierre Faye. It most certainly applies to Audiberti.

By the conventions governing established practices and conditioning our reflexes, the contact between author and reader aimed at by the written text is possible only by means of a tacit "complicity" which is normally taken for granted and which has been considered indispensable for the transmission of the linguistic message. But the author Jacques Audiberti makes no apparent attempt to "help" his reader become a participant in this intelligence pact. At least not on those terms, not through conditioned reflexes and ready-made cultural values.

To a large extent, the Audibertian text calls for potential initiates who are willing to free themselves of their cultural conditioning, of their logic and of their "rational" minds, in order to enter into the experience of a major intuitive order: the recoding of the "system." As we have indicated in the preceding chapter, the "system" is, as far as Audiberti can see, the code of classical humanism. His perception of the cultural-literary status quo in those terms is apparent in his writings as early as 1942. It is in *La Nouvelle origine* that we first notice the evidence of the contemplated "Abhumanist" project. It is in that short essay of 1942 that he calls for a "revocabulation." From that point onward, the totality of his production seems a monumental display of an effort to achieve precisely that goal. To "revocabulate" is to change the code, to institute a new code. Indeed it is to institute the "Abhumanist" code. In this perspective, the Audibertian message is unambiguous and impeccably coherent. The Abhumanist code asserts itself as a set of well-defined positions most of which are stated more or less explicitly in his essay *L'Abhumanisme*. These are positions opening immense perspectives, covering global, well integrated issues: The Abhumanist code is antiAristotelian and antiintellectual (cf. Essay on Giordano Bruno, in *L'Abhumanisme*, pp. 209-26). It is the code for values that counter the tendency to valorize abstract concepts, the tendency to valorize a language that moves farther and farther away from the natural sources of life, to valorize science over the occult, the West over the East, "Voltaire, Giraudoux, France, Valéry" over Villon, Rabelais, Molière, Péguy and Claudel. (*Ibid.*, pp. 50-51); the capital over the countryside: "Occidentale, accidentelle, la France, pourtant, c'est la betterave" (*Ibid.*, p. 51); technological progress over the occult; De Broglie over Robert-Houdin and so forth.

Accordingly, the code is for "recuperating" analogous values in the language of literature: "Par la vertue de sa forme naturelle, la forme fixe, symétrique, rimée, évoque une cadence préhistorique, une rumeur répétitive, le langage d'avant les mots" (*Ibid.*, p. 95). This is also the code that valorizes patois over formal French, argot over the language of the Boulevard: "Sous le français royal et boulevardier, l'argot s'efforce d'être [. . .] un dialecte abhumaniste ou se transcriraient le poil et le poids des choses au niveau pantruchard de la fibre spontanée de la vie en sa crudité" (*Ibid.*, p. 57). It is the code that valorizes baroque exuberance over conciseness and reduction: "Que fait la vieille Parque valéryste? Elle attache ensemble les mots français les plus précis, les plus choisis. A quels fins? Pour qu'ils se vident les uns dans les autres par dubitative succion et délétère contagion. Le discours ainsi modulé se situe à de telles distances du préjugé, du besoin, du service et du désir qu'il se dissipe, au bout du compte dans le miroir de l'absence" (*Ibid.*, pp. 50-51).

Having examined the character of the impulse for the Abhuman, in the author's mythopoeic processes, and the structures of the Abhumanist message, in the preceding chapter, we can now see that between *La Nouvelle origine* and *L'Abhumanisme* Audiberti's texts reveal an awareness of the necessity to create a system of signs for some sort of "cosmic poetics." It is questionable that his intuitions can be directly related to current research in semiotics. Audiberti had never serious enough ambitions that we could compare with the "scientific" character of semiotic studies. But in his intuitive logic, we can see that the solutions he opts for are of the type usually attributed to the Structuralist school of thought. Interestingly, Camille Bryen reports that in a reference to *L'Ouvre-boîte*, Jean Grenier wrote a letter to him in which he stated, "vous avez anticipé sur le structuralisme . . ."[4] As Michel Giroud pointed out, Audiberti could see the problem of a universal language with a modern vision: "chaque langue est un fragment d'une langue générale inconnue; on aurait ainsi la résolution des contradictions: une particularisation universelle; . . ."[5]

And it is no doubt in this area that we must assess his merit. In his monumental enterprise, Audiberti contemplates a system of signs that is based on a radical departure from the *denotative* code of the typically French value system. The processes we examined in the preceding chapter under the designation of regressive modulations are eloquent testimony to his aspiration for some type of a *"connotative"* code to use Jean Cohen's term. The Abhumanist code will be a lexicon where words are defined by the psychic or emotive content, not the cognitive content. It will be able to take into account the primitive forces of nature, the mystery of religion, the rural and popular sources of the French culture, the affective properties of language. This code will forever display the unmistakable seal of Audiberti's personal culture. For it will forever be, as Georges Perros said on a recent occasion, "cette langue espéranto qui n'est ni celle des poètes ni celle des philosophes, ni celle de personne mais qui tend à être celle de tout le monde. Qui ouvre sur un prolétariat triomphant, flambant neuf, rendu à sa nature, qui est d'éternité [. . .] Les mots faucheurs—au sens labour—d'Audiberti. Qui profitent du goût de terre. De la mer [. . .] entre le latin et l'argot, Côté titi du Midi passant rue Saint-Denis [. . .][6]

It is to be hoped that the code will be the key to resolving future enigmas of our planet's destiny: The suggestion of such a possibility is strong in the notorious tin-can opener metaphor introduced by the *"colloque abhumaniste"* with Camille Bryen, in *L'Ouvre-boîte*. The tin-can opener is offered as a precious tool, indispensible for survival. In a more recent *"colloque,"* in an interview between Michel Butor and Camille Bryen, the author of *6,810,000 litres d'eau par seconde* offered an updated interpretation of the Abhumanistic metaphor by reiterating in his own terms its special message for modern man:

Nous nous promenons aujourd'hui dans une sorte de gigantesque supermarché, entre des murs de boîtes que nous ne savons pas ouvrir, et nous avons besoin pour ces boîtes d'instruments qui vont nous permettre de délivrer tout ce qui peut être à l'intérieur, et nous-mêmes qui sommes de plus en plus enfermés à l'intérieur de certaines boîtes.[7]

Notes and References

Chapter One

1. Cf. Michel Corvin, *Le Théâtre nouveau en France* (Paris: P.U.F., 1966). Martin Esslin, *Théâtre de l'Absurde* (Paris: Buchet-Chastel, 1963). Pierre Voltz, *La Comédie* (Paris: Armand Colin, 1964).
2. Quoted by Michel Giroud, *Audiberti* (Paris: Editions Universitaires, 1967), p. 7.
3. Jean Cassou, preface in Jeanyves Guérin, *Le Théâtre d'Audiberti et le baroque* (Paris: Klincksieck, 1976), p. 11.
4. Quoted by André Deslandes, *Audiberti* (Paris: Gallimard, 1964), p. 21.
5. André Pieyre de Mandiargues, "A Force de mots." *N.R.F.*, Dec. 1, 1965, p. 1066.
6. Quoted by Deslandes, *op. cit.*, p. 16.
7. *L'Ouvre-boîte* No. 5, 1975, p. 9.
8. Quoted by Deslandes, *op. cit.*, pp. 29–30.
9. Antipolis is the ancient name of Antibes.
10. Michel Giroud, *op. cit.*, pp. 15–16.
11. Quoted by Michel Giroud, *op. cit.*, p. 13.
12. Michel Giroud, *Audiberti* (Paris: Seghers [Poètes d'audjourd'hui], 1973), p. 73.
13. Gaston Bouthoul, "Le Rempart d'Audiberti." *N.R.F.*, Dec. 1, 1965, p. 1055.
14. Quoted by André Deslandes, *op. cit.*, p. 46.
15. Paul Guth, *Quarante contre un* (Paris: Denoel, 1951), p. 29.
16. Gaston Bonheur, "L'Unique spectateur." *N.R.F.*, Dec. 1, 1965, p. 1025.
17. Michel Giroud, *op. cit.*, 1973, p. 82.
18. *Ibid.*, p. 85.
19. Cf. Georges Vitaly, "Pour un théâtre de choc." *Revue théâtrale* 7, April–May 1948, 33–38.
20. Cf. Jeanyves Guérin, *op. cit.*, pp. 221–30.
21. Unpublished letter quoted by Michel Giroud, *op. cit.*, pp. 7–8.
22. *L'ouvre-boîte* No. 4, 1957, p. 17.
23. Michel Giroud, *op. cit.*, 1967, p. 85.
24. Monique Pantel, "Comme on ferme les volets." *N.R.F.*, Dec. 1, 1965, p. 1016.

Chapter Two

1. Etiemble, "Lettre au vieux compagnon de route," *Poètes ou faiseurs?* (Paris: Gallimard, 1966), p. 367.
2. André Bourin, "Avec Audiberti," *Paru*, 53 (Aug.–Sept. 1949), 14.
3. André Pieyre de Mandiargues, preface to *Race des Hommes* (Paris: Gallimard [coll. Poésie], 1968), p. 10.
4. *Ibid.*
5. Gabriel Bounoure, "Audiberti," *Marelles sur le parvis* (Paris: Plon, 1958), p. 292.
6. *Ibid.*, p. 294.
7. Maurice Chapelan, "Audiberti ou l'apprenti sorcier." *N.R.F.*, 330 (Aug. 1941), 235.
8. André Deslandes, *op. cit.*, p. 161.
9. Alain Bosquet, "Audiberti, burlesque et mystique." *N.R.F.*, 136 (Avril 1964), 677.
10. Jeanyves Guérin, "Audiberti poète et paysan . . . du Danube," *Démarches poétiques et linguistiques* (Saint-Etienne: C.I.E.R.E.C., 1977), p. 230.
11. Michel Giroud, *op. cit.*, 1973, p. 55.
12. Alain Bosquet, *op. cit.*, p. 678
13. See letter to Lévi-Strauss, *L'Ouvre Boîte* No. 4, p. 17.
14. Jeanyves Guérin, "Audiberti poète et paysan . . . du Danube," *op. cit.*, p. 229.
15. Michel Giroud, *op. cit.*, 1967, p. 85.
16. Georges Perros, "Micmac Audiberti," preface to *Poésies* (Paris: Gallimard, 1976), p. 9.
17. Michel Giroud, *op. cit.*, 1967, p. 72.
18. Michel Giroud, *op. cit.* 1973, p. 20.

Chapter Three

1. André Deslandes, *op. cit.*, p. 51.
2. Henry Amer, "Audiberti, romancier de l'incarnation." *N.R.F.*, 46 (Oct. 1956), 685.
3. *Ibid.*, p. 688.
4. *Ibid.*, p. 689.
5. Henry Amer, *op. cit.*, *N.R.F.* 47 (Nov. 1956), 886–89.
6. *Ibid.*, p. 890.
7. André Deslandes, *op. cit.*, p. 90.
8. *Ibid.*, p. 99.
9. *Ibid.*
10. Michel Giroud, *op. cit.* 1967, p. 55.
11. *Ibid.*

12. *Ibid.*, p. 66.
13. Michel Giroud, *op. cit.* 1973, p. 13.

Chapter Four

1. For a detailed analysis of Audiberti's Catholic background and his sympathies with Judaism, see Jeanyves Guérin, *Le Théâtre d'Audiberti et le baroque, op. cit.* pp. 48–62 and André Pieyre de Mandiarques, *Troisième Belvedère, op. cit.* p. 249.

2. Based on a remark W. B. Yeats once made concerning Jarry's *Ubu roi;* George Wellwarth sees even the motif of evil, in Audiberti, in terms of the *Savage God,* the malignant power of the cosmos. He further suggests that "the conflict between paganism and Christianity, and the presence of a primordial spirit of evil in human affairs," are themes Audiberti derived from Artaud's. [Cf. *The Theater of Protest and Paradox* (New York: New York University Press, 1964), pp. 73–84.]

3. Cf. Paul-Louis Mignon, *Le Théâtre d'aujourd'hui* de A à Z (Paris: Michel Brient & Cie., 1966), p. 31.

4. Jean Rousselot, *Poètes français d'aujourd'hui* (Paris: Seghers, 1959), pp. 124–30.

5. Pierre Seghers, "Avant-propos," in Jean Rousselot, *op. cit.*, pp. 7–9.

6. The monster referred to as "bête du Gévaudan" is presumed to be the notorious beast which, from 1765 to 1787, terrorized the Gévaudan countryside. According to a legend, the beast devoured dozens of people before it was killed by a peasant [cf. H. Pourrat, *Histoire fidèle de la bête du Gévaudan* (Chermont-Ferrand: Ed. de l'Epervier, 1946)].

7. Cf. a similar ritual involving a boar, in *Le Soldat Dioclès.*

8. Quoted by Christian Millau, in "Jacques Audiberti brasseur de désordre, est un homme d'ordre." *Fémina-Théâtre*, Oct. 1956, p. 28.

9. The play was first produced under the title *La Hobereaute*, at the Festival des Nuits de Bourgogne, in 1956, with Jean le Poulain directing.

Chapter Five

1. André Breton's preface to Lautréamont's *Ouvres complètes* (Paris: Corti, 1958), p. 43.

2. In his interview with Georges Charbonnier, the author confirmed what is more or less evident in the play as a reference to the precolumbian divinity depicted as the "Serpent bird": "Quoat-Quoat est le nom approximatif d'un dieu Méxicain (le dieu Quetzacoatl ou quelque chose comme cela . . .)" (*Entretiens*, p. 93)

3. In an interesting comparison with the Camusian concept of "L'Homme révolté," George Wellwarth made this observation: "Amedée is the rebel-hero of whom Camus speaks. He finds his death—and, paradoxically, his

freedom at the same time—by taking his stand and saying thus far will he permit himself to be driven and no further." ("Jacques Audiberti: The Drama of the Savage God," *The Theater of Protest and Paradox*, p. 77)

4. *Altamima* is the only one of Audiberti's plays in which the comic element is totally absent, both from situations and from language.

5. This brings to mind a classification of Audiberti's female characters in terms of the *Femme-enfant/sorcière* typology borrowed from Benjamin Péret's *Anthologie de l'amour sublime* (cf. review of Madeleine Hage's thesis *Le Mythe de la femme dans le théâtre d'Audiberti*, in *L'Ouvre-boîte* No. 5)

6. Jean-Marie Auzias, *op. cit.*, p. 13.

7. Cf. "L'Interdit et la transgression," particularly pp. 33–104, in *L'Erotisme* (Minuit, 1957).

Chapter Six

1. Christian Millau, *op. cit.*, p. 28.

2. Marcel Raymond, *De Baudelaire au Surréalisme* (Paris: Corti, 1963), p. 45.

3. Antonin Artaud, "Le Théâtre et son double," *Oeuvres complètes* IV. Paris: Gallimard, 1964), p. 14.

4. *Ibid.*, p. 11.

5. Quoted by Jeanyves Guérin, *Le Théâtre d'Audiberti et le baroque* (Paris: Klincksieck, 1976), p. 93.

6. This text was first published in 1965 (*N.R.F.* 156, Dec. 1965, 972–99).

7. The text of this one-act sketch is part of *Les Médecins ne sont pas des plombiers*. It was produced for the first time at the Noctambules, in April 1950, with André Reybaz directing.

8. Michel Giroud, *op. cit.* 1967, p. 51.

9. Jeanyves Guérin, *op. cit.*, p. 82.

10. René Etiemble, *op. cit.*, p. 360.

11. Jeanyves Guérin, *op. cit.*, p. 107.

12. The last chapter of *L'Abhumanisme* is an essay on Giordano Bruno in whose life and "martyrdom" Audiberti sees a model Abhumanist.

Chapter Seven

1. Quoted by André Deslandes, *op. cit.*, p. 214.

2. Jacques Lemarchand, "Non, Marcel Achard, le public n'est pas infaillible . . . mais il finira par aimer *La Brigitta*." *Le Figaro littéraire*, 859, Oct. 6, 1962, 22.

3. Jean-Michel de Renaitour, *Le Théâtre à Paris en 1959* (Paris: Editions du Scorpion, 1960), p. 203.

4. Pierre Marcabru, review of *La Mégère Apprivorisée, Arts* 460, Oct. 16, 1957, 4.

5. Quoted by André Deslandes, *op. cit.*, p. 215.

6. Michel Giroud, *op. cit.* 1967, p. 27.

7. Jean-Marie Auzias, "Le Retour au baroque chez Audiberti." *Baroque* VI (1973), 16.

8. Paul Surer, *op. cit.*, p. 432.

9. Jean Tortel, *Clefs pour la littérature* (Paris: Seghers, 1971), p. 159.

10. The period pieces are the following: *L'Ampelour, La Fête noire, Quoat-Quoat, Les Femmes du Boeuf, Le Mal court, Le Cavalier seul, Altanima, Opéra parlé, La Fourmi dans le corps, Le Soldat Dioclès, Coeur à cuir, Les Patients, Bâton et ruban, La Guérite, La Guillotine.*

11. "Michel Butor interroge Camille Bryen," *L'Ouvre-boîte* No. 8 (Nov. 1977), p. 28.

12. Jeanyves-Guérin, *Le Théâtre d'Audiberti et le baroque. Op. cit.*, p. 75.

13. Michel Giroud, *op. cit.*, 1967, p. 97.

14. Guy Dumur, "Audiberti ou le théâtre en liberté." *Théâtre populaire*, 31-32 (Sept.-Oct. 1958), 159.

15. Dominique Fernandez, "Audiberti, l'intolérant." *Arc* 9, 1959, 52.

16. Jeanyves Guérin, *Le Théâtre d'Audiberti et le baroque, op. cit.*, p. 188.

17. See "Sire le mot," in *Le Théâtre d'Audiberti et le baroque*, pp. 171-88.

18. It is significant that the Cerisy colloquium on Audiberti, in 1976, was planned under the sign "Audiberti, le trouble-fête."

19. Jeanyves Guérin, *op. cit.*, p. 186.

20. Program of *Le Mal court*, Théâtre La Bruyère, 1955.

Chapter Eight

1. André Pieyre de Mandiargues, *op. cit.*, p. 249.

2. Henry Amer, *op. cit.*, p. 887.

3. Cf. André Reybaz, *Têtes d'affiche* (Paris: Table Ronde, 1975). Marcel Maréchal, *La Mise en théâtre* (Paris: Union Générale d'Edition (10/18, 1975). Claire Goll, *La Poursuite du vent* (Paris: Olivier Orban, 1976). We also gain interesting insights into the Audibertian vision, particularly some aspects of his teratology as influenced by painting, from studies on Leonor Fini's art, such as Marcel Brion, *Leonor Fini* (Paris: J. J. Pauvert, 1973), and Constantin Jelensky, *Leonor Fini* (Lauzanne: Fontaine, 1968).

4. Despite his correspondence with Claude Levi-Strauss and exchanges with him on questions related to poetry and literature in general, it is unlikely that Audiberti was ever introduced to the famous anthropologist's system of thought. His knowledge of the latter's writings was limited to *Tristes tropiques*, the one book by Levi-Strauss known to be his most readable work.

5. Michel Giroud, *op. cit.*, p. 173, p. 25.

6. Georges Perros, "Le Micmac Audiberti," *op. cit.*, pp. 12-14.

7. "Michel Butor interroge Camille Bryen," *L'Ouvre-boîte* No. 8, p. 27.

Selected Bibliography

PRIMARY SOURCES

1. Poetry

L'Empire et la Trappe. Paris: Gallimard, 1969. (Rpt. of the original edition: *L'Empire et la Trappe.* Paris: Librairie du Carrefour, 1930)

Race des Hommes. Paris: Gallimard, 1969. (preface by André Pieyre de Mandiargues. Poems of the original edition, *Race des Hommes.* Paris: N.R.F., 1937)

Poésies. Paris: Gallimard, 1976. (Rpt. in one volume of three original editions: 1) *Des Tonnes de semence.* Paris: N.R.F., 1941. 2) *Toujours.* Paris: Gallimard, 1943. 3) *La Pluie sur les Boulevards.* Angers: Au Masque d'or, 1950)

Vive guitare. Paris: Laffont, 1946.

Rempart. Paris: Gallimard, 1953.

Lagune hérissée. Paris: Les Cent et une, 1958 (Text by Audiberti and original lithos by J. Carzou).

Ange aux entrailles. Paris: Gallimard, 1964.

2. Essays

Paroles d'éclaircissement. Aurillac: Editions de la pomme de sapin, 1940.

La Nouvelle Origine. Paris: N.R.F., 1942.

Les Médecins ne sont pas des plombiers. Paris: Gallimard, 1948.

L'Ouvre-boîte (in collaboration with Camille Bryen). Paris: Gallimard, 1952.

Molière. Paris: Editions de l'Arche, 1954.

Le Retour du Calife (in Les Mille et une Nuits). Paris: Editions de la Bibliothèque mondiale, 1954.

L'Abhumanisme. Paris: Gallimard, 1955.

Les Enfants naturels. Paris: Fasquelle, 1956.

3. Narrative Fiction

Abraxas. Paris: Gallimard, 1965. (Rpt. of the original edition, *Abraxas:* Paris, Gallimard, 1938)

Septième. Paris: Gallimard, 1939.

Urujac. Paris: Gallimard, 1941.

Carnage. Paris: Gallimard, 1942.

La Fin du Monde. Paris: Le Temps perdu, 1943.

Le Retour du divin. Paris: Gallimard, 1943.

La Nâ. Paris: Gallimard, 1944.
Monorail. Paris: Gallimard, 1964. (Rpt. of the original edition, *Monorail*, Fribourg-Paris: Egloff, 1947)
Talent. Fribourg-Paris: Egloff, 1947.
L'Opéra du monde. Paris: Fasquelle, 1947.
Le Victorieux. Paris: Gallimard, 1947.
Cent jours. Paris: Gallimard, 1950.
Le Maître de Milan. Paris: Gallimard, 1950.
Marie Dubois. Paris: Gallimard, 1952.
Les Jardins et les fleuves. Paris: Gallimard, 1954.
La Beauté de l'amour. Paris: Gallimard, 1955.
La Poupée. Paris: Gallimard, 1956.
Le Sabbat ressussité par Leonor Fini. Paris: Société des Amis des Livres, 1957.
L'Infanticide préconisé. Paris: Gallimard, 1958.
Les Tombeaux ferment mal. Paris: Gallimard, 1963.
Dimanche m'attend. Paris: Gallimard, 1965.

4. Theater

La Bête noire. Paris: Les Quatre Vents, 1945.
Théâtre, tome I; Quoat-Quoat; L'Ampelour; Les Femmes du Boeuf; Le Mal court. Paris: Gallimard, 1948.
Théâtre, tome II; La Fête noire; Pucelle; Les Naturels du Bordelais. Paris: Gallimard, 1952.
Le Cavalier seul. Paris: Gallimard, 1955.
Théâtre, tome III; La Logeuse; Opéra parlé; Le Ouallou; Altanima. Paris: Gallimard, 1956.
La Hobereaute. Paris: *Paris-Théâtre*, No. 746 (n.p.)
L'Effet Glapion. Paris: Gallimard, 1959.
Théâtre, tome IV; Coeur à cuir; Le Soldat Dioclès; La Fourmi dans le corps; Les Patients; L'Armoire classique; Un Bel enfant. Paris: Gallimard, 1961.
Théâtre, tome V; Pomme, Pomme, Pomme; Bâton et ruban; Boutique fermée; La Brigitta. Paris: Gallimard, 1962.
La Guérite. *N.R.F.* No. 132 (Dec. 1, 1963)
La Guillotine. *N.R.F.* No. 142, 143 (Oct. 1, Nov. 1, 1964)
La Poupée; Comédie en six tableaux. Paris: Gallimard, 1969.

5. Interviews

AUDIBERTI, JACQUES. *Entretiens avec Georges Charbonnier.* Paris: Gallimard, 1965.
GILLOIS, ANDRÉ. *Qui êtes-vous?* Paris: Gallimard, 1953, 25–33.
JELENSKI, K. A. "Entretien avec Audiberti sur le métier d'écrivain," *Preuves.* Nov. 1965, pp. 3–5.

MITHOIS, MARCEL. "Un Auteur dramatique vous parle: Jacques Audiberti," *Réalités*, No. 199, Aug. 1962, 76–82.

SECONDARY SOURCES

1. Monographs

DESLANDES, ANDRÉ. *Audiberti*. Paris: Gallimard (Coll. Bibliothèque Idéale), 1964. First major comprehensive study on the author's works as of that date. Particularly useful for a section of brief summaries covering a complete inventory of major works.

GIROUD, MICHEL. *Audiberti*. Paris: Editions Universitaires (Coll. classiques du XXe Siècle), 1967. Excellent, detailed study covering all aspects of the author's complete works. Includes a wealth of updated bibliographical information.

GIROUD, MICHEL. *Audiberti*. Paris: Seghers (Coll. Poètes d'Aujourd'hui), 1973. Incisive, well documented study on the author's writing techniques and on the origins and evolution of his poetic style. The critical exposé is followed by a selection of poems, including a few previously unpublished ones.

GUÉRIN, JEANYVES. *Le Théâtre d'Audiberti et le baroque*. Paris: Klincksieck (Coll. Théâtre d'Aujourd'hui), 1976. A thorough, extensively documented, thematic study on the author's theater. Particularly valuable for its analyses of the author's religious references, of his philosophy of history and of his philosophy of language. Uncommonly rich in biographical data.

Hommage à Jacques Audiberti. Textes inédits. Témoignages-hommages. Etudes. *N.R.F.*, No. 156 (Dec. 1965).

2. General Studies on Theater

BEIGBEDER, MARC. *Le Théâtre en France depuis la libération*. Paris: Bordas, 1959.

CORVIN, MICHEL. *Le Théâtre nouveau en France*. Paris: Presses Universitaires de France, 1966.

GROSSVOGEL, DAVID I. *The Self-conscious Stage in Modern Drama*. New York: College University Press, 1958.

GUICHARNAUD, JACQUES. *Modern French Theater from Giraudoux to Beckett*. New Haven: Yale University Press, 1961.

KEMP, ROBERT. *La Vie du théâtre*. Paris: Albin Michel, 1956.

MARÉCHAL, MARCEL. *La Mise en théâtre*. Paris: Union générale d'édition (10/18), 1975

PRONKO, LEONARD CABELL. *Avant-garde: The Experimental Theater in France*. Berkeley and Los Angeles: University of California Press, 1966.

REYBAZ, ANDRÉ. *Têtes d'affiche*. Paris: La Table Ronde, 1975.

SANDIER, GILLES. *Théâtre et combat*. Paris: Stock, 1970.

SERREAU, GENEVÌEVE. *Histoire du nouveau théâtre.* Paris: N.R.F. (Coll. Idées), 1966.

SURER, PAUL. *Cinquante ans de théâtre.* Paris: S.E.D.E.S., 1969.

VOLTZ, PIERRE. *La Comédie.* Paris: A. Collin (Coll. U), 1964.

WELLWARTH, GEORGE E. *The Theater of Protest and Paradox.* New York: New York University Press, 1964.

3. Major Critical Articles

A. On Audiberti's poetry

BOSQUET, ALAIN. "Audiberti, burlesque et mystique," *N.R.F.*, 12e année, No. 136 (April 1964), 675-80.

BOUNOURE, GABRIEL. "Audiberti," in *Marelles sur le parvis*, essai de critique poétique. Paris: Plon, 1958, 292-94.

BOUNOURE, GABRIEL. "Jacques Audiberti." *La Revue du Caire*, 18e année, No. 181, June 1955, 355 -64.

CASSOU, JEAN. "L'Empire et la Trappe." *Nouvelles littéraires*, Dec. 13, 1930.

CHAPELAN, MAURICE. "Audiberti, ou l'apprenti sorcier." *N.R.F.*, 29ème année, LV, No. 330 (Aug. 1941), 232-38.

CORNELL, KENNETH. "Audiberti and obscurity." *Yale French Studies*, II, 2 (Fourth study), 100 -04.

GUÉRIN, JEANYVES. "Audiberti poète et paysan . . . du Danube." *Démarches poétiques et linguistiques.* Saint-Etienne: C.I.E.R.E.C., 1977, 225-32.

MANDIARGUES, ANDRÉ PIEYRE DE. *Troisième Belvédère.* Paris: Gallimard, 1971, 247-54.

ROUSSELOT, JEAN. "Audiberti." *Les Nouveaux poètes français. Panorama critique.* Paris: Seghers, 1959, 138-45.

B. On Audiberti's novels

AMER, HENRY. "Audiberti toujours." *N.R.F.*, No. 156 (Dec. 1965), pp. 1086-93.

AMER, HENRY. "Audiberti, romancier de l'incarnation." *La Nouvelle N.R.F.*, VIII (Oct. 1956), 685 -93 and IX (Nov. 1956), 883 -90. Penetrating, comprehensive study on Audiberti's novels.

ARLAND, MARCEL. "*Abraxas* par Audiberti," *N.R.F.*, Dec. 1938, 1037 -40.

ARLAND, MARCEL. "Urujac," *N.R.F.*, 1941 (t.55, 214-15)

ARLAND, MARCEL. "En Compagnie d'Audiberti," *Lettres de France.* Paris: Albin Michel, 1951, 199-208.

ARLAND, MARCEL. "La Saison du roman" in *Nouvelles lettres de France.* Paris: Albin Michel, 1954, 202 -07. (Review of *Marie Dubois*)

DRIEU LA ROCHELLE. "Audiberti." *N.R.F.*, No. 343 (Sept. 1942), 358 -63.

FERNANDEZ, DOMINIQUE. "Audiberti, l'intolérant." *Arc* No. 9, 1959, 49 -52.

KANTERS, ROBERT. "Les Tombeaux ferment mal." *Le Figaro Littéraire*, 21 (Sept. 1963). Review of *Les Tombeaux ferment mal.*

POULET, ROBERT. "Jacques Audiberti," in *La Lanterne magique*, I. Paris: Debresse, 1956, 188-92. Excellent analysis of *Les Jardins et les fleuves.*

150 JACQUES AUDIBERTI

SAUREL, RENÉE. "Audiberti le prodigue," *Cahiers M.R. -J. -L. B.*, 7ème Cahier 1954, 49–52. Review of *Les Jardins et les fleuves*.

C. On Audiberti's theater
AUZIAS, JEAN-MARIE. "Le Retour au baroque chez Audiberti." *Baroque*, No. VI (1973), 13–17. Brilliant analysis of Audiberti's major accomplishments as related to major, influential events of postRenaissance culture.
BARATIER, JACQUES. "Audiberti." *Biblio*, XXXIe année, No. 3 (March 1963), 8–9.
CISMARU, ALFRED. "Audiberti's Quest for Eden." *Renascence*, XIX, 3 (Spring 1967), 122–30.
DUMUR, GUY. "Audiberti ou le théâtre en liberté." *Théâtre Populaire*, No. 31 (Sept. 1958), 153–66. First comprehensive review of Audiberti's theater, offering qualified, praising assessments.
FOLLAIN, JEAN. "Le baroque douloureux d'Audiberti." *Baroque*, No. VI (1973), 7–12.
FRIPPIAT, YVES-MARIE. "Le Pouvoir dans le théâtre d'Audiberti." *Les Lettres romanes*, No. XXVII (1973), 248–98.
LEMARCHAND, JACQUES. "Audiberti dramaturge." *Biblio*, XXXIe année (March 1963), 6–7.
MÉLÈSE, PIERRE. "Avant-garde Theater in France." *Theater Annual*, XVIII (1961), 1–16.
MILLAU, CHRISTIAN. "Jacques Audiberti, brasseur de désordre, est un homme d'ordre." *Femina-Théâtre*, Oct. 1956, 23–28.
ROUBINE, JEAN-JACQUES. "Audiberti et Molière." *Revue d'histoire littéraire de la France*, No. 5–6 (Sept.–Dec. 1973), 1081–93.

Index

151